The Nashville Number System

by

Chas Williams

Edition 6

ISBN 0-9630906-0-7

"Finally a `How to' on the *Nashville Number System*! What used to be inside information in the studios of Music City USA is now made available to the public. Chas Williams has spent hours of intense research and interviewing to bring to you the unique art of writing music in numbers, instead of traditional manuscript. This system has saved literally hours of studio and rehearsal time in Nashville, and even across America. All I can say is thank you, Chas for an interesting, well-written, and `Timely' contribution to the music world."

- Lura Foster

"This is the most complete version of the *Nashville Number System* as I've ever seen. Chas Williams has a full understanding of the number system, and this book is an excellent source to begin learning the *Nashville Number System*."

- Charlie McCoy

"The *Nashville Number System*, by Chas Williams, is a book I really needed back in 1983 when I moved to Nashville for a recording career. I had to learn it bit by bit, trying to keep up. It can save you alot of time and embarrassing moments."

- Mark O'Connor

"This book seems to be the definitive answer to those desiring to understand the *Nashville Number System*. In addition to a brief history of the system, the book details several versions exemplifying the variety of styles used. I highly recommend it for anyone involved or seeking to become involved in the Nashville music community."

- Brent Rowan

" Chas Williams' book is as valid in Boston as in Nashville. Berklee is using the book to prepare students for the recording industry."

- Robert Stanton
Assistant Professor-Berklee College of Music

"After looking through *The Nashville Number System*, it would be in my opinion, the most informative book for learning this system and being able to apply your own way of using this method."

- Eddie Bayers

Table of Contents

Introduction

The *Nashville Number System* is a method of transcribing music so that a song can be understood and performed by musicians. Nashville chord charts substitute numbers for the chord letter symbols found in traditional music notation. Rhythmic and dynamic notations, as well as chord voicing symbols from formal music are used in conjunction with symbols developed uniquely by Nashville musicians.

Since the middle ages, musicians have substituted Roman numerals for chord letters. However, around 1957, Neal Matthews, a member of the *Jordanaires,* originated the idea of substituting numbers for notes. Working several recording sessions a day forced Neal to devise a method of writing vocal parts so that the *Jordanaires* wouldn't have to commit tremendous amounts of material to memory. Neal said he was familiar with the system of shape notes used by gospel quartets in the 30's and 40's, which used a different shape for each note of the major scale. He began writing vocal charts substituting numbers for the shape notes and developed his own system of writing music with numbers.

In the early 60's Charlie McCoy, Wayne Moss, and David Briggs noticed the unique approach that Neal and the Jordanaires used to map out a song on paper. So, Charlie expanded and adapted Neal's number system to focus on the instrumental portion of a song. From McCoy, Moss, and Briggs, the idea of substituting numbers for chord letters quickly spread among the other session players in Nashville. Musicians used the number system to chart out an entire song on one piece of paper while hearing a demo of the tune for the first time. This innovative number system has become the standard method of music notation in Nashville.

One of the benefits of a number chart is that it can be played in any key without transposing or rewriting the chart into a different key. A chart's numbers maintain their same relationship with a song's chord changes regardless of the key. For example, if Dolly Parton sings *I Saw the Light* in the key of **C**, Johnny Cash might sing the same song lower, in the key of **G**. If they use identical arrangements, the same Nashville number chart of *I Saw the Light* would work for both Dolly's and Johnny's performance. As well, dictation of a song from a tape or radio is very easy because you don't need to know a key to write down the correct chord changes and melodies. This is especially nice for those of us not blessed with perfect pitch.

Over the years, country music has expanded to include many complex rhythm patterns and chord structures. Phrasing and rhythms from pop, rock, jazz, blues, cajun, and reggae have been incorporated into the music of country artists. As a result, musicians have combined traditional notation symbols with Nashville chord charts so complex music can be interpreted and played precisely. There are symbols and notations unique to the *Nashville Number System* not found anywhere else. For example, the *Diamond* ◇ means to strike and hold a chord for the designated amount of time.

Oddly enough, there is no one definitive version of the *Nashville Number System*. Many musicians use different symbols and notations to express the same musical idea. For example, the diamond may be written: ◇5 ◇ over 5 and 5 over ◇ . Also, some people indicate a split bar (a measure with more than one chord change) with a diagonal slash: ***1/5***, whereas others enclose the measure with parentheses ***(15)***, or in a box **15** . Some people underline the split bar: ***15***.

The number system is the common language for communicating music in Nashville. If you are a songwriter, it is a valuable tool to help you express your ideas, so other musicians can understand and translate them effectively. If you are paying for a demo of your song, a well prepared chart of the tune will communicate your musical ideas precisely and save studio time. On the other hand, if you are playing on a demo, you may need to write a chart for yourself without knowing what key the song will be played.

This book explores some of the different styles and techniques of writing number charts that are used by some of the most respected musicians in Nashville. I will teach you how to translate your song into a Nashville number chart by applying some fundamental music theory. You can learn to write your chart with any degree of detail you desire; a basic road map number chart open to interpretation, or one with a highly detailed arrangement.

Also, I describe the *Nashville Number System* spoken language . You will be able to discuss *number charts* and talk chord progressions with other musicians. When somebody yells, "Fifteen Eleven"across a stage, you'll know it's chords and not a football score. As well, this book teaches terms used to describe feel and style for different types of music.

Included are number charts for seven country standards; each song's chart handwritten by some of Nashville's most influential musicians. Each musician wrote charts from the same record. Featured are Patsy Cline's version of *Crazy* and Ray Price's version of *Crazy Arms.* You will see first hand the charts that are read by the bands for *Prime Time Country, Hee Haw,* and the *Grand Ole Opry*. As a result, you'll be able to compare some of the different styles of notation and symbols available for use in your number charts. These types of charts represent the kinds of numbering techniques that you are liable to encounter in almost all of the major recording and television studios, clubs, showcases, rehearsal halls, and other situations where music is performed in Nashville.

In addition is the cd ***1511*** . This disc contains 9 original compositions. I have written charts for each song, and one by one, discuss why I use different *number system* tools and concepts. As a result, you will be able to *see, hear and feel* how these charts work.

So, whether you are a songwriter trying to get your material performed, a band leader learning songs from a record, or a producer teaching an arrangement in the studio, the *Nashville Number System* is a great way of presenting your songs and musical ideas.

Major Scales and Number Substitution Table

Key	Whole Step		Whole Step		Half Step	Whole Step		Whole Step		Whole Step		Half Step
1	♯1 or ♭2	2	♯2 or ♭3	3	4	♯4 or ♭5	5	♯5 or ♭6	6	♯6 or ♭7	7	1
A	A♯ or B♭	B	B♯ or C	C♯	D	D♯ or E♭	E	E♯ or F	F♯	F♯♯ or G	G♯	A
A♯	A♯♯ or B	B♯	B♯♯ or C♯	C♯♯	D♯	D♯♯ or E	E♯	E♯♯ or F♯	F♯♯	F♯♯♯ or G♯	G♯♯	A♯
B♭	B or C♭	C	C♯ or D♭	D	E♭	E or F♭	F	F♯ or G♭	G	G♯ or A♭	A	B♭
B	B♯ or C	C♯	C♯♯ or D	D♯	E	E♯ or F	F♯	F♯♯ or G	G♯	G♯♯ or A	A♯	B
C	C♯ or D♭	D	D♯ or E♭	E	F	F♯ or G♭	G	G♯ or A♭	A	A♯ or B♭	B	C
C♯	C♯♯ or D	D♯	D♯♯ or E	E♯	F♯	F♯♯ or G	G♯	G♯♯ or A	A♯	A♯♯ or B	B♯	C♯
D♭	D or E♭♭	E♭	E or F♭	F	G♭	G or A♭♭	A♭	A or B♭♭	B♭	B or C♭	C	D♭
D	D♯ or E♭	E	E♯ or F	F♯	G	G♯ or A♭	A	A♯ or B♭	B	B♯ or C	C♯	D
D♯	D♯♯ or E	E♯	E♯♯ or F♯	F♯♯	G♯	G♯♯ or A	A♯	A♯♯ or B	B♯	B♯♯ or C♯	C♯♯	D♯
E♭	E or F♭	F	F♯ or G♭	G	A♭	A or B♭♭	B♭	B or C♭	C	C♯ or D♭	D	E♭
E	E♯ or F	F♯	F♯♯ or G	G♯	A	A♯ or B♭	B	B♯ or C	C♯	C♯♯ or D	D♯	E
F	F♯ or G♭	G	G♯ or A♭	A	B♭	B or C♭	C	C♯ or D♭	D	D♯ or E♭	E	F
F♯	F♯♯ or G	G♯	G♯♯ or A	A♯	B	B♯ or C	C♯	C♯♯ or D	D♯	D♯♯ or E	E♯	F♯
G♭	G or A♭♭	A♭	A or B♭♭	B♭	C♭	C or D♭♭	D♭	D or E♭♭	E♭	E or F♭	F	G♭
G	G♯ or A♭	A	A♯ or B♭	B	C	C♯ or D♭	D	D♯ or E♭	E	E♯ or F	F♯	G
G♯	G♯♯ or A	A♯	A♯♯ or B	B♯	C♯	C♯♯ or D	D♯	D♯♯ or E	E♯	E♯♯ or F♯	F♯♯	G♯
A♭	A or B♭♭	B♭	B or C♭	C	D♭	D or E♭♭	E♭	E or F♭	F	F♯ or G♭	G	A♭

Using the Major Scale and Number Substitution Table

Use the Major Scale Number Substitution Table on page 7 to determine what number your chord is, or the chord for which you have a number. The Step Formula for finding the major scale is at the top of the chart. Each major scale is spelled from the left to right with large letters. Chromatic half steps between each whole step degree of the scale are in small letters.

Use this table the same way you would use the table in a road atlas to find the distance between two cities. Find your key in the far left column. Search the horizontal row of the key you are in for the chord whose number you need to find. When you find the chord, from there follow the column upward to discover the corresponding number.

Likewise, if you need to know what chord a certain number is, find the number at the top of the table. Then, follow that column down until you reach the horizontal spelling of the scale for your key. The two columns should intersect at the correct chord.

If you are playing your song on guitar and using a capo, assign numbers to chords as if you're not using a capo at all. For instance, if your song is in the key of **D**, but you're capoed to the second fret, you will be playing with chord forms as if you're in the key of **C**. So you may read the table as if you are in the key of **C** instead of **D**. The numbers will be the same for both keys.

One more thing, though we know that **B#** and **C** are the same note, correct alphabetical spelling of the A major scale dictates that the **#2** must be a **B#**. Since there is no **B#** in the chromatic scale, for simplicity, in the key of **A**, call **C** the **b3**. Adhering to the same spelling rule, the ***#6*** in **A** should be **F##** (F double sharp). **F##** is the same note as **G**, so we'll use **G** as the **b7** in the key of **A**, instead of **F##** as the **#6**.

The Major Scale Derivation

Chromatic Scale

The chromatic scale is composed of all 12 notes within an octave, beginning with and including the tonic, or *1*, for which the scale is named. To play an **A** chromatic scale on guitar, start with the open fifth string, **A**, and play the note on every fret upward until you reach the next **A** note on the 12th fret, one octave above.

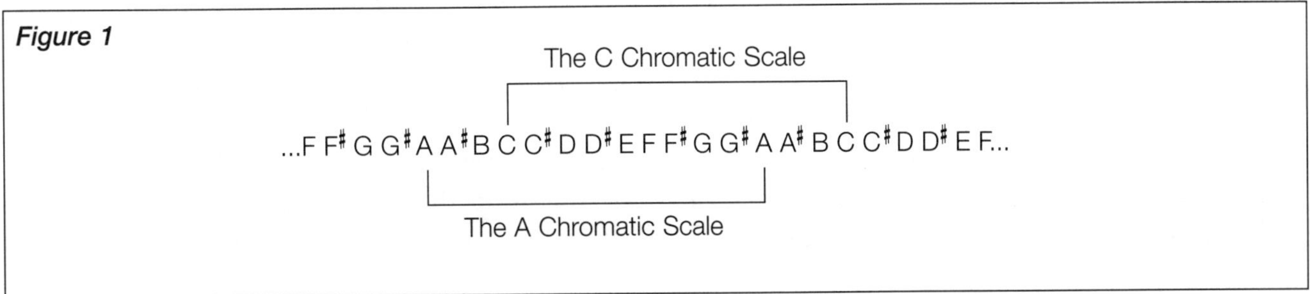

Intervals

An interval is the distance between two notes. **A** to **A♯** (**A** Sharp) is a half step, or minor 2nd interval. **A** to **B** is a whole step, or major 2nd interval. Two half steps equal a whole step, regardless of the spelling. For instance, there is no note between **E** and **F**, so **E** to **F** is only a half step, while **E** to **F♯** is a whole step. The same holds true for the interval between **B** and **C**. There is no other note between **B** and **C**, so **B** to **C** represents a half step. **C** to **C♯** also represents a half step, so a whole step up from **B** is **C♯**. One half step down from **B** is **B*b*** (**B** flat). Whenever notes or chords move up or down in a series of half steps, it is called, moving "chromatically."

Step Formula

The step formula is a way of extracting a major scale from the chromatic scale. It tells which intervals to use to determine each degree of the major scale. The step formula remains constant, so a major scale can be found, beginning with the tonic, or *1* of any key.

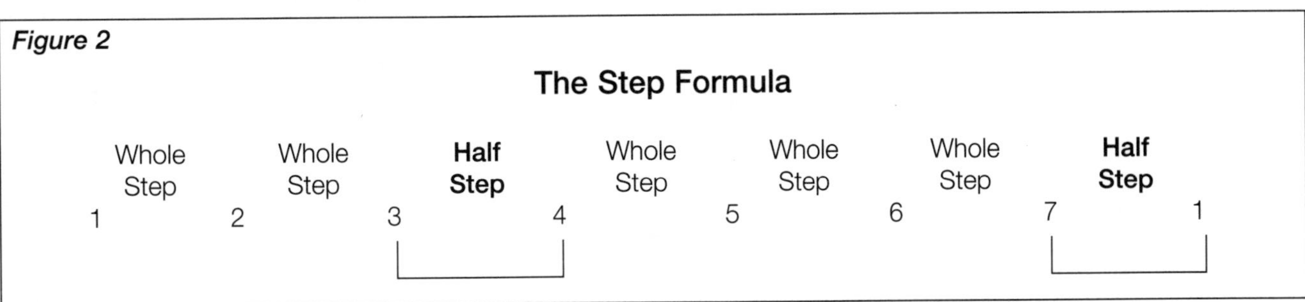

The Major Scale and Number Substitution

The major scale consists of seven notes, which are derived alphabetically from the chromatic scale by applying the step formula. Flip back to page 9 and refer to the Step Formula in Figure 2 as you read the following paragraphs.

To spell a major scale, begin with the "tonic," or ***1***, for which the scale is named. This will become the name of the key we are working in. You can spell a major scale in any key, although for our example, we will show you how to spell the **A** major scale. Therefore, **A** is the tonic, or *1*. Applying the step formula, we find that the second note or degree of the scale must be a whole step up from the ***1***. Spelling alphabetically up the chromatic scale one whole step, we see that **B** is the second degree, or **2** of the **A** major scale. To find the third degree of the **A** major scale, spell ahead a whole step from the **2**. **B** to **C** is only a half step, so a whole step from **B** is **C♯**. Therefore, **C♯** is the third degree, or **3** of the **A** major scale. A question arises, though... isn't **C♯** the same note as **D♭**? Well, yes, it sounds the same, but remember, we're spelling alphabetically, so the whole step up from **B** is spelled **C♯** instead of **D♭**.

We look again at the step formula to determine that the interval between the third and fourth notes of the scale needs to be a half step. So, we spell ahead one half step from **C♯**, the **3**, to **D**, which will be the fourth degree, or **4**, in the key of **A**. Next, according to the step formula, we must spell ahead one whole step from **D**, the **4**, to determine the **5** note of the A major scale. Therefore, **E** is the **5**. Likewise, the **6** is a whole step from the **5**. **E** to **F** is only one half step, so a whole step from **E** is **F♯**. **F♯** is the **6**. One alphabetical whole step farther, we find that G is the seventh degree, or 7 of the A major scale. Finally, according to the step formula, from the ***7***, spell ahead one half step to reach the ***1*** again, which will be one octave above the **A** note where we began. So, by spelling alphabetically up the chromatic scale, beginning with the tonic of the key you are in, and using intervals which are predetermined by the step formula, we've written the **A** major scale.

Pick any note and you can sing its major scale with "Do Re Mi". For example, Do is ***1***, Re is ***2***, Mi is ***3***, and so forth, until you reach Do, or ***1***, one octave higher.

Figure 3

Do	Re	Mi	Fa	So	La	Ti	Do
1	2	3	4	5	6	7	1

The step formula remains constant, regardless of which key you're spelling. In every major scale, there will be a half step between ***Mi*** and ***Fa*** and a half step between the ***Ti*** and ***Do***. There will be a whole step interval between all the other degrees of the major scale.

The Nashville Numbers

In the Nashville system, numbers assigned to each step of the major scale represent chords as well as single notes. In the key of **A**, we have the major scale **A B C♯ D E F♯ G♯**. This major scale become chords ***1 2 3 4 5 6 7***. **A** is the ***1*** chord and **G♯** is the ***7*** chord. You've probably heard of a " **I, IV, V** " blues progression. It's the same in Nashville. In the key of **A**: **I, IV** and **V** is **A**, **D** and **E**, but it's written with numbers ***1, 4*** and ***5*** instead of Roman Numerals. This may seem too simple, but the Nashville numbers are assigned directly to the major scale for the key that your song is in. It gets better.

Still in the key of **A**, what if our song goes to a **G** chord instead of a **G♯** chord? If we flat or lower the **G♯**, or ***7*** chord, one half step we have the **G**, or ***b7*** chord, we need for our song. Once more, in the key of **A**, how do we determine what number to assign a **C** chord? Well, we know that **C♯** is the ***3*** chord, and **C** is one half step below **C♯**. So, one half step below the ***3*** chord is the ***b3*** or "flat three" chord. Likewise, what is the ***b6*** chord in the key of **A**? Simply determine the ***6*** chord and flat it one half step. **F♯** is the ***6*** , therefore **F** is the ***b6*** chord. On the other hand, to find the ***♯4*** or "sharp four" chord, determine the ***4*** chord and raise or sharp it one half step. In the key of **A, D** is the ***4*** chord, therefore **D♯** is the ***♯4*** or "sharp four" chord.

Some musicians like to place the sharp or flat sign after the chord number. For example, ***b7*** and ***♯4*** may be written ***7b*** and ***4♯*** called "seven flat and four sharp." This is because the number is substituted for the chord's proper name. You would say "**Eb**" not "**bE**."

However, I like to think of a number not only as a chord's identification and proper name, but also as its ***function*** within a progression. When analyzing traditional jazz harmony, you use Roman numerals to identify a chord's function in all keys. A substitute chord like a $\flat II^7$ has the flat sign in front of the chord to show how the chord was altered from the major scale. Also, what if you had a $\flat 7^{\flat 9}$? Isn't it confusing to write $7\flat^{\flat 9}$ and call it a "seven flat, flat nine"?

The 1 chord is the tonic and is built on the first note of its major scale. It establishes the key and is usually the final resting point for the progression. The V^7 chord is called the dominant . It carries tension and makes you want to resolve back to the **I**. These are chord functions. All chords function to move a progression forward ultimately to a final rest at the **I** chord.

In Nashville, we use numbers instead of Roman numerals. The numbers still dictate function within a progression and the flat or sharp sign before a number shows what you did to that chord with relationship to the major scale.

Another question: Why write a ***♯4*** chord instead of a ***b5*** chord since they are the same? Likewise, why a ***b7*** instead of a ***♯6*** ? Most of the time you use flatted chords ***b2, b3, b5, b6*** and ***b7***. However, in a progression that is moving up in half steps or "chromatically", a passing chord may be written as a sharp. For a progression moving chromatically downward, the passing chord may be a flat. For example, when moving chromatically from the ***1*** to the ***2***, you write ***1 ♯1 2*** . On the other hand, in the case of the ***2*** down to the ***1***, you write ***2 b2 1***.

Relative Minor

The ***6*** note of any major scale is the ***1***, or tonic, of that scale's relative minor key. For example, in the key **C**, the ***6*** is **A**. Therefore **A** minor is the relative minor of the key of **C** major. The same notes are used for each scale, except that the **A** relative minor scale begins with **A** and the half steps fall between the ***2*** and ***3***, and the ***5*** and ***6***.

Figure 4

The A Relative Minor Scale and the Relative Minor Step Formula

A		B		C		D		E		F		G		A
1		2		3		4		5		6		7		1
	Whole Step		**Half Step**		Whole Step		Whole Step		**Half Step**		Whole Step		Whole Step	

Take, for instance, *The House of the Rising Sun*, in **A** minor. **A** minor is the tonic or ***1*** minor chord.

Figure 5

E Relative Minor Scale

E	F♯	G	A	B	C	D	E
1	2	3	4	5	6	7	1

Study Figure 5 for a moment to see how the relative minor step formula is used to construct the **E** relative minor scale. Notice that this **E** minor scale uses the same notes as the **G** major scale.

Having said all that... In Nashville, *most of the time*, for a song in a minor key, the chord chart will be written as if in the relative major key. Even if **A** minor sounds like the actual tonic, or ***1*** minor chord, the chart is written as if in the key of **C** major. In which case the **A** minor chord is written as the ***6*** minor. It is therefore, important to know how to find the relative major of a minor key. Here's how to do it.

To determine the relative major of a minor key, spell upward from the tonic note for which the minor scale is named, 3 half steps. In Figure 4 (which uses the **A** minor scale) spell upward 3 half steps from the ***1*** (**A→A♯**, **A♯→B** ,**B→C**) to find that **C** is the relative major of the key of **A** minor. If you were writing a chart for *The House of the Rising Sun* (which is in **A** minor) you would write it in the relative major (which is **C**), where **A** minor is the ***6*** minor and $\mathbf{E}^{7}$ is the $\boldsymbol{3}^{7}$.

Another example is if you were playing *Ghost Riders In the Sky* in the key of **E** minor. Then, the tonic chord sounds like **E** minor. However, you find the relative major (**G**) and write the chart in the key of **G**. The first chord of the song is **E** minor and will be written as **6-**. The **G** chord in the chorus will be written as ***1***.

Chord Symbols

In addition to assigning each chord a number, we must designate whether the chord is a major or minor, and if it carries a seventh, a major seventh, etc.

A major chord needs no symbol. The number by itself always means that it is a basic major chord. Minor chords carry a minus sign to the right of the chord number, ***6-*** . You may also use a small ***m*** for minor, but that can sometimes be confused with major.

Chord voicing (ninths, sixths, sevenths, etc.) appear as smaller numbers to the upper right of the chord, 5^7.

Some chords are played with a different bass note, for example, a **4** chord with a **5** note in the bass. This is written as a fraction, $\frac{4}{5}$, and called a "four over five." For example, progressions with the moving bass lines like the first four measures of Mr. Bojangles can be written as shown below in Figure 6.

Figure 6

$1 \quad \frac{1}{7} \quad 6\text{-}^{7} \quad \frac{1}{5}$

Another common walk down is ***4*** down to ***1***. Figure 7.

Figure 7

$4 \quad \frac{1}{3} \quad 2\text{-}^{7} \quad 1$

Figure 8

Chord Symbol Chart

Major	1^{Δ}
Major Seventh	1^{Δ} , $1^{\text{maj.7}}$
Major Ninth	$1^{\Delta 9}$, $1^{\text{maj.9}}$
Dominant Seventh	1^{7}
Sixth	1^{6}
Ninth	1^{9}
Major add 9	$1^{\text{add 9}}$, $1^{♀}$
Minor	6- , 6^{m} , $6^{\text{min.}}$
Minor Seventh	6-^{7} , 6^{m7} , $6^{\text{min.7}}$
Minor Sixth	6-^{6} , 6^{m6} , $6^{\text{min.6}}$
Minor Major Seventh	6-^{Δ} , $6^{\text{m}\Delta}$, $6\text{-}^{\text{maj.7}}$
Augmented	5+
Augmented Seventh	$5+^{7}$
Diminished	$^{\#}4^{\circ}$
Diminished Seventh	$^{\#}4^{\circ 7}$
Half Diminished	7-^{7b5} , $7^{ø}$
Seven with a flat 9	$5^{7\,b9}$
Eleven	5^{11}
Thirteen	5^{13}

♀ is my own shorthand for *add 9*. It's fast, but is not officially recognized by the rest of the world.

Time

Time Signatures

A time signature must be denoted before a chart is begun. The time signature tells how many beats may fit in one measure as well as the time value of each beat.

Take, for example, a time signature of $\frac{4}{4}$ (read as "four, four"). The top number dictates that four beats will be counted in each measure. The bottom number specifies that each of the 4 beats will be counted with a quarter note value. In other words, one measure of $\frac{4}{4}$ will contain a total of four quarter note beats. Time signatures, however, do not indicate the tempo (speed) at which the beats will be counted and played.

Common Time Signatures

$\frac{4}{4}$ 4 beats per measure, a quarter note gets one beat (ex.: *On the Other Hand*, by Randy Travis)

$\frac{2}{4}$ 2 beats per measure, a quarter note gets one beat (ex.: *Rocky Top*, by The Osborne Brothers)

$\frac{3}{4}$ 3 beats per measure, a quarter note gets one beat (ex.: *Rose Colored Glasses*, by John Conlee)

$\frac{6}{8}$ 6 beats per measure, an eighth note gets one beat (ex.: *Mammas, Don't Let Your Babies Grow Up to Be Cowboys*, by Waylon Jennings)

Although a time signature establishes the number of basic beats a measure will receive, a measure may be subdivided into as many rhythmic variations as called for by the song. However, the totalled rythmic values of the notes in a measure may not exceed or be less than the total value designated by the time signature.

Note Values

One whole note (𝅝) equals two half notes (𝅗𝅥); one half note (𝅗𝅥) equals two quarter notes (♩); one quarter note (♩) equals two eighth notes (♪); and one eighth note (♪) equals two sixteenth notes (𝅘𝅥𝅯). Figure 9 below illustrates the relationship between these five basic note shapes (which represent five basic time values). Each note value is grouped for one complete measure of $\frac{4}{4}$ time.

Figure 9

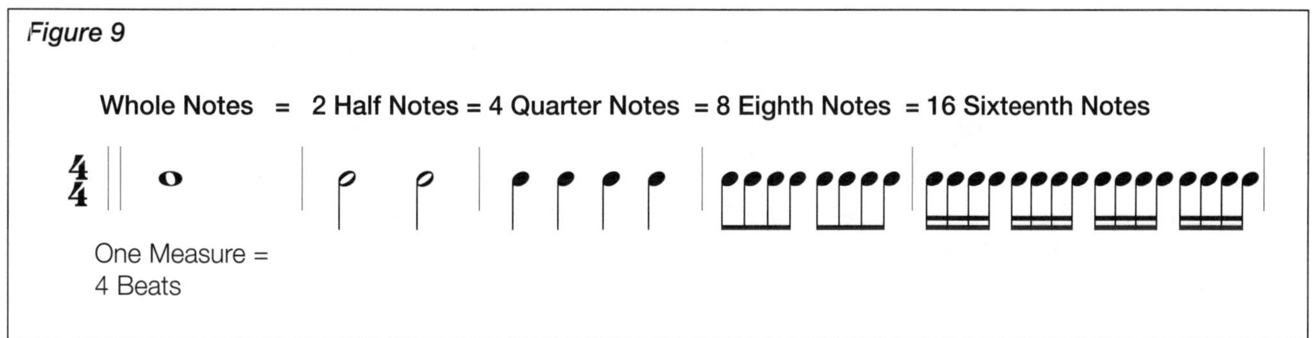

When counting a measure of $\frac{4}{4}$, you count "1,2,3,4." If you are counting eighth notes, you count "1 and, 2 and, 3 and, 4 and." Each number is an eighth note down-beat, while the "and" stands for an eighth note upbeat. So, one beat of $\frac{4}{4}$ gets "1 and," or 2 eighth notes. If you are counting sixteenth notes, count a measure of $\frac{4}{4}$ as shown below in Figure 10.

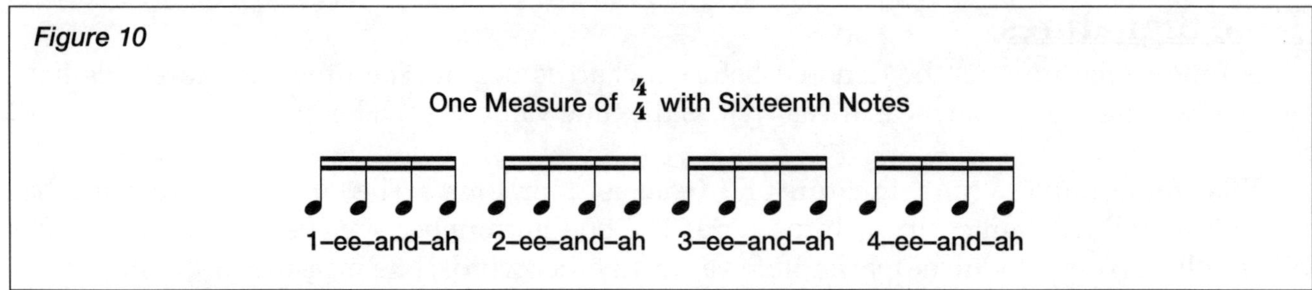

Figure 10

In each of the examples that follow in Figure 11 the measures are subdivided differently, but they all have the total number of time as dictated by the time signature.

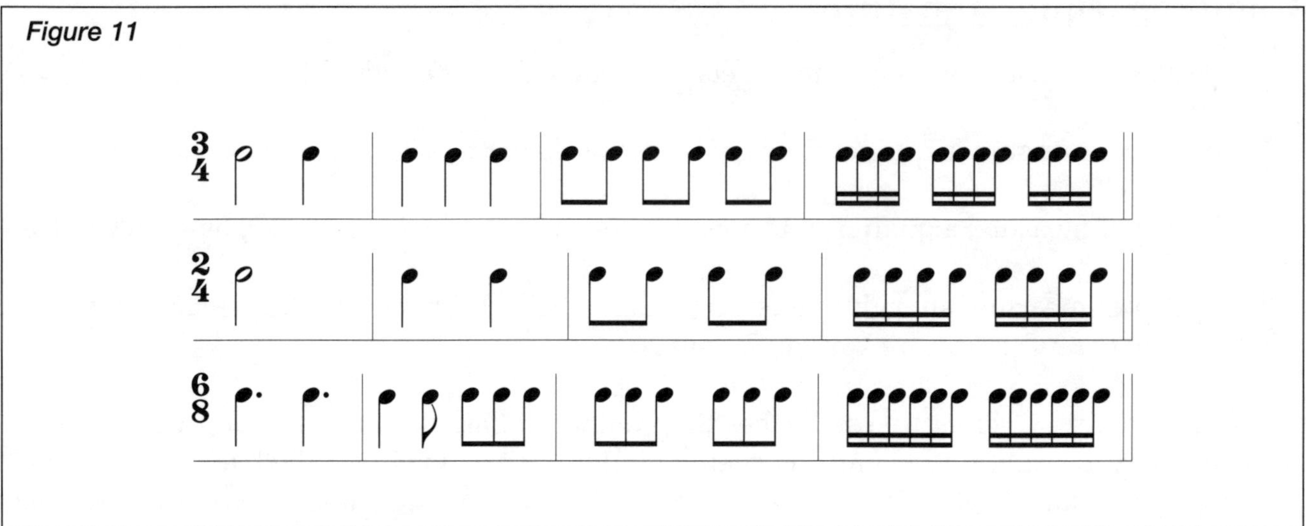

Figure 11

Rests

When there is no musical activity going on within a measure, time must still be counted and notated with the proper value of rest.

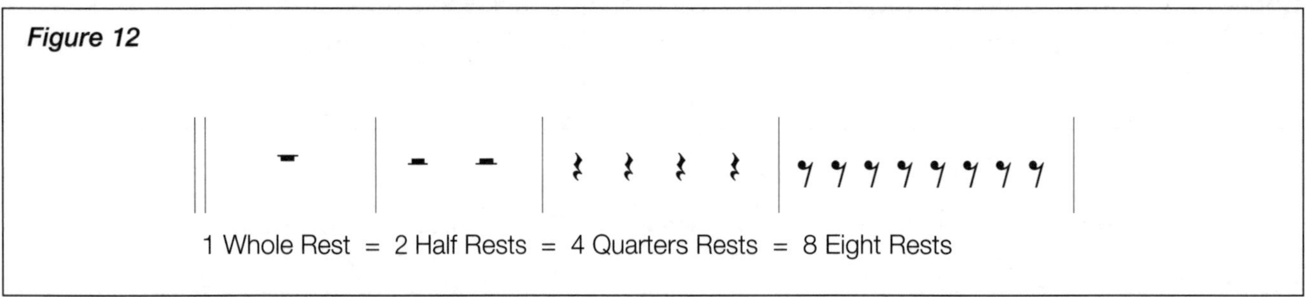

Figure 12

In formal music, whole note rests and half note rests are drawn on separate staff lines. Since there are no staff lines in the Nashville system, we use only a portion of the staff line to differentiate whole note from the half note rests (Figure 12). Also, be careful to keep quarter note rests from looking like 3's and eighth note rests from looking like 7's.

Dotted Note

A dot after a note or rest increases the time value of that note by one half of the note dotted.

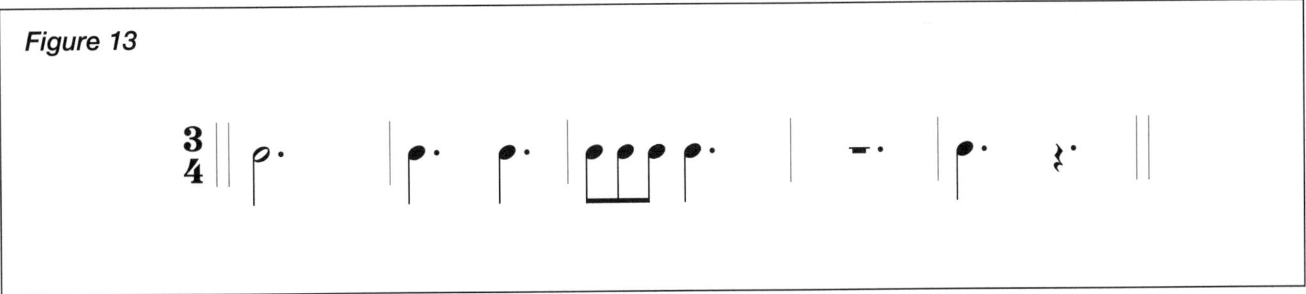
Figure 13

Triplets

An eighth note triplet equals one quarter note. There would be 4 eighth note triplets in a measure of $\frac{4}{4}$.

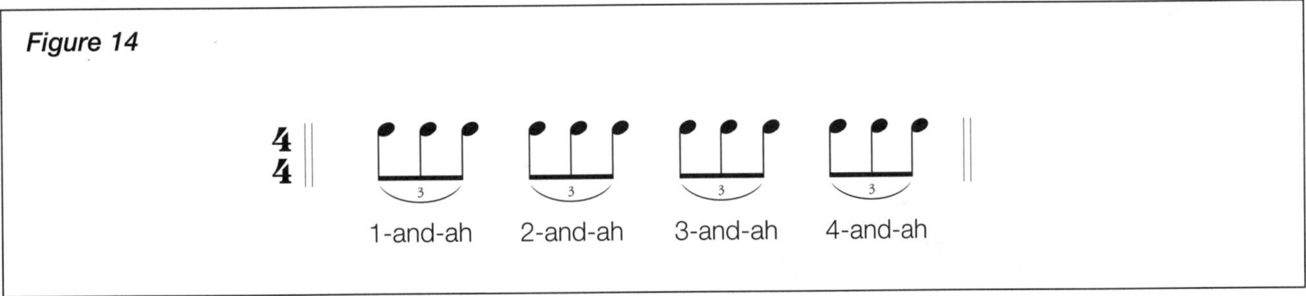

Figure 14

Blueberry Hill and *Unchained Melody* are counted with a slower $\frac{4}{4}$ but have a fast triplet or $\frac{12}{8}$ feel. If not all the notes of a triplet figure are struck, use an eighth rest in the triplet figure.

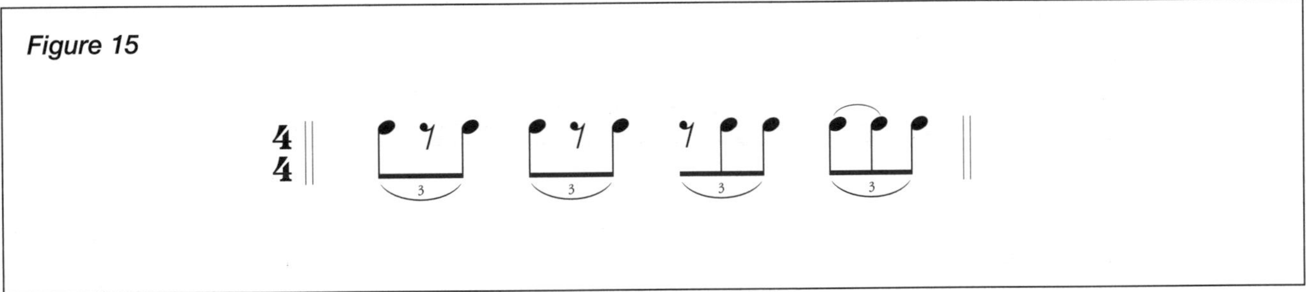
Figure 15

Quarter Note Triplet

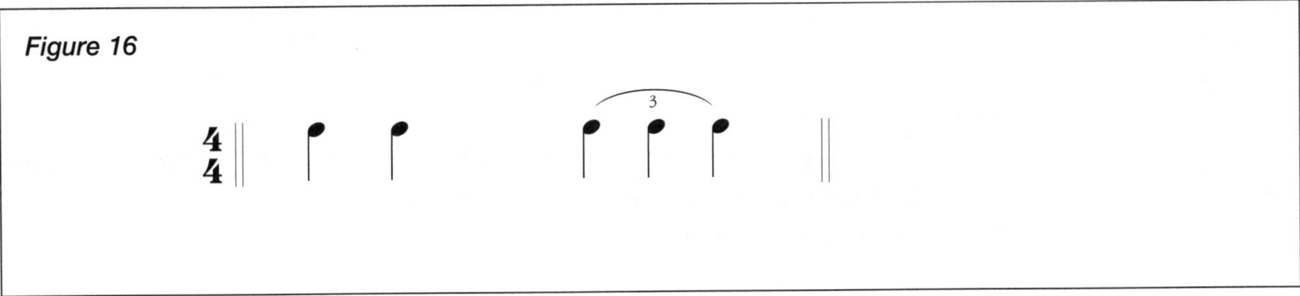
Figure 16

A quarter note triplet equals two beats and has a syncopated feel.

Tied Notes

A tied note is struck once and held for the duration of both notes together.

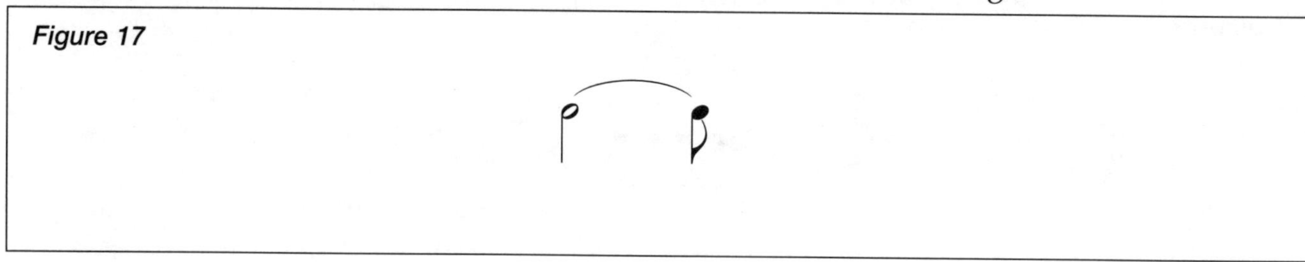

Figure 17

In Figure 17, the note is struck once and held for 2 1/2 beats. If the two notes are a different pitch, the first note is bent smoothly to the second. The second note is not restruck.

Split Bars

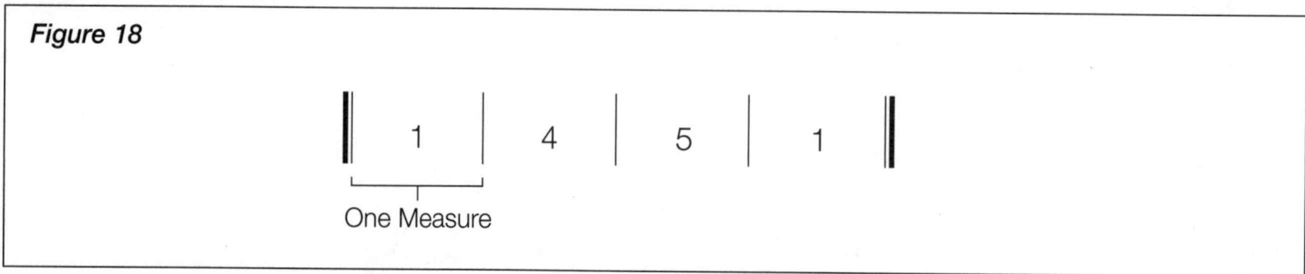

Figure 18

In Figure 18, there is one bar, or measure between each divider mark. However, in the *Nashville Number System*, the divider marks for each measure are imaginary and not written, because they are easily confused with the number *1*. When a chord number is written, it automatically lasts one measure. Usually there are four measures per line. In Nashville, the line in Figure 18 would be written: ***1 4 5 1***

In Figure 19, measures can be subdivided like so:

Figure 19

$\frac{4}{4}$ ‖ 1 5   1 5 1   1 5 1   1 5   1 4 5 1

Or into whatever combinations may fit your song. When more than one chord is written within a measure, the chord numbers are underlined. These measures are called split bars. When there is an uneven number of beats per chord, small hash marks over the chord show how many beats each chord gets. When there are two chords in a measure and each gets 2 beats, no hash marks are necessary. The same applies if there are 4 separate chords in a measure of $\frac{4}{4}$. They automatically get one beat each and no hash marks are needed. If a split bar has a syncopated rhythm, or attacks that aren't on the basic downbeat, you may enclose the measure in a box and write the rhythmic phrase in notation above the chord changes.

Some people like to use parentheses around a split bar or divide the measure with a diagonal slash. The slash, however, can make a split bar look like a chord with a different bass note. I like to underline evenly split bars and put more rhythmically complex bars in a box.

Figure 20

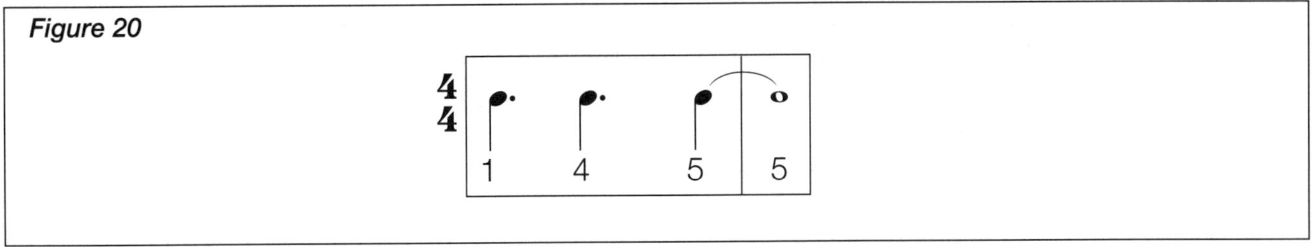

When you use rythmic notation, you may box in your split bars. In Figure 20, the **4** chord is pushed or anticipated. It is struck on the "and" of beat 2. Then, the last beat in the first bar is tied to the next measure. The symbol > is an abbreviation for the push, or anticipation, and goes over the chord being pushed. So, another way to write the above example could be:

Figure 21

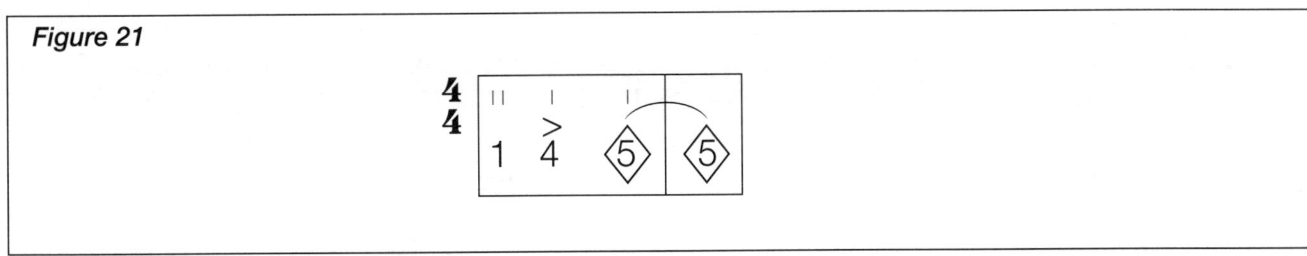

The diamond in Figure 21 is the sign for strike and hold for the designated duration. We'll talk more about diamonds in the section on dynamics.

Here's another rhythmic measure:

Figure 22

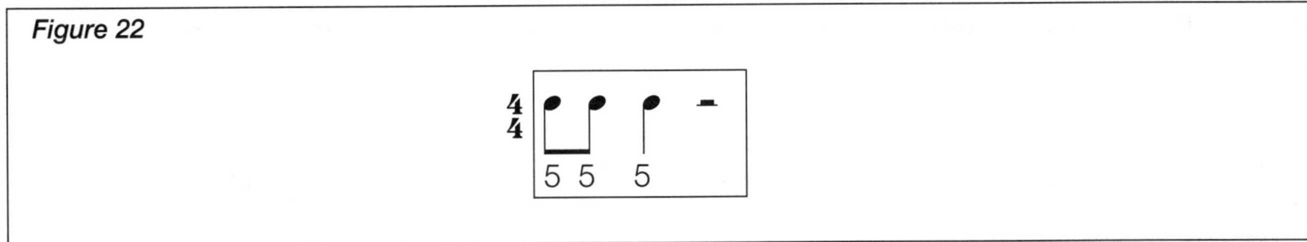

In Figure 22, the **5** chord is struck with two eighth notes and a quarter note, then muted with a half note rest for the remaining two beats of the measure.

New Time Signature

In formal notation, you may change the time signature by writing the new signature in parentheses before the measure that changes; then resume by inserting the original time signature in parentheses in front of it's next measure.

A lot of songs will have a phrase that contains an extra half measure (Figure 23, bar 3).

Figure 23

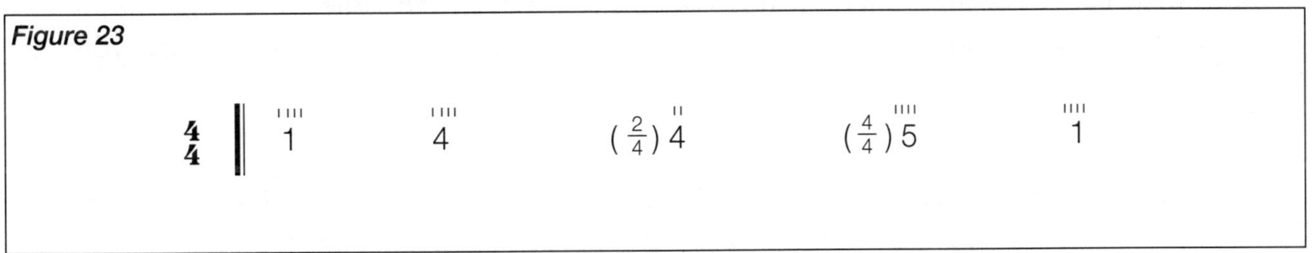

The time signature can change, to allow a song's phrasing to go for an extra half measure before changing back to the original signature. In this case, it's easy to put a $\frac{2}{4}$ bar in a box with two hash marks above the number, like in Figure 24. Figure 24 contains the same line as Figure 23. The boxed measures are $\frac{2}{4}$ and get only 2 beats, then $\frac{4}{4}$ time automatically resumes without having to re-enter another time signature.

The chord changes from Figure 23 could also be written as in Figure 24a or 24b:

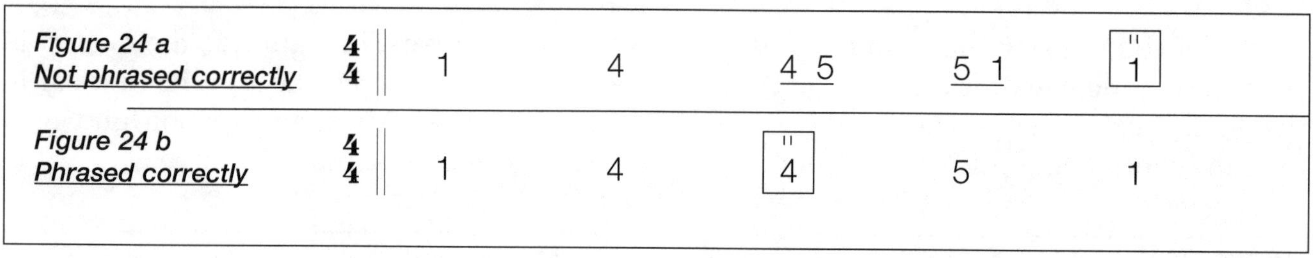

	Time					
Figure 24 a *Not phrased correctly*	$\frac{4}{4}$	1	4	4 5	5 1	[II 1]
Figure 24 b *Phrased correctly*	$\frac{4}{4}$	1	4	[II 4]	5	1

The difference between Figures 24a and 24b is the phrasing. A musical or vocal phrase should start at the beginning of a new measure. In Figure 24a, *if* the 4 chord in the first half of the third measure is the end of a phrase, and the 5 chord in the second half of the same measure is the beginning of a new phrase, write your chart as in Figure 24b.

A good example of a time signature change and an extra measure is in the chorus of *Mammas Don't Let Your Babies Grow Up To Be Cowboys*, by Waylon Jennings.

Figure 25

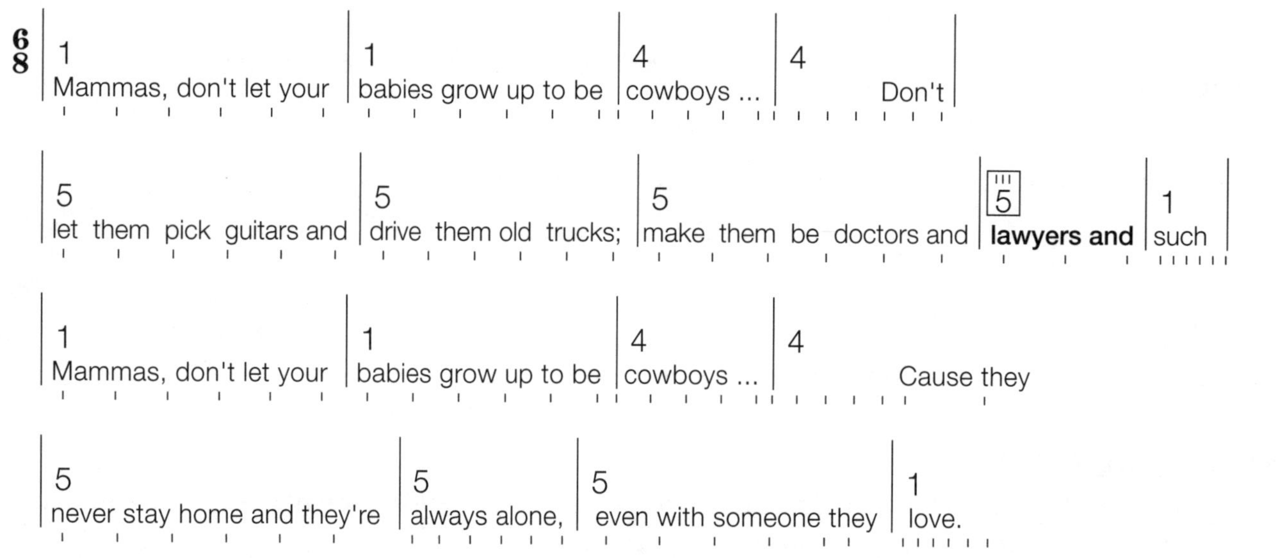

$\frac{6}{8}$
| 1 Mammas, don't let your | 1 babies grow up to be | 4 cowboys ... | 4 Don't |

| 5 let them pick guitars and | 5 drive them old trucks; | 5 make them be doctors and | [III 5] **lawyers and** | 1 such |

| 1 Mammas, don't let your | 1 babies grow up to be | 4 cowboys ... | 4 Cause they

| 5 never stay home and they're | 5 always alone, | 5 even with someone they | 1 love.

Melody and word phrasing suggest that the eighth measure in Figure 25 is an extension of the phrase that began in the *seventh measure*. So, the **5** in the *eighth measure* of the figure should be written as one bar of $\frac{3}{8}$. The ninth measure of the figure resumes with $\frac{6}{8}$ time.

The second line of *Mamma's*, from Figure 25, ends up with a total of four and a half measures, and should be written as in Figure 26.

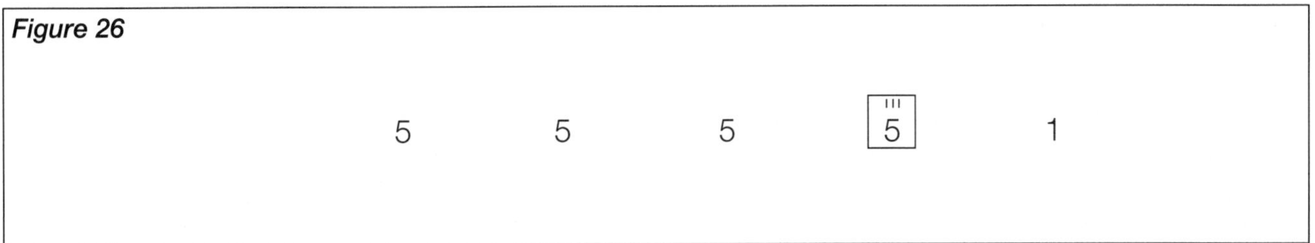

Melody Notation

The number system can apply to single notes, as well as chords. Numbers are assigned to different notes in a scale the same way they are assigned to different chords. Rhythmic notation is written beneath the number to show the time value of each note. An arrow ↑ or ↓ can show which direction an interval moves from the previous note.

Figure 27

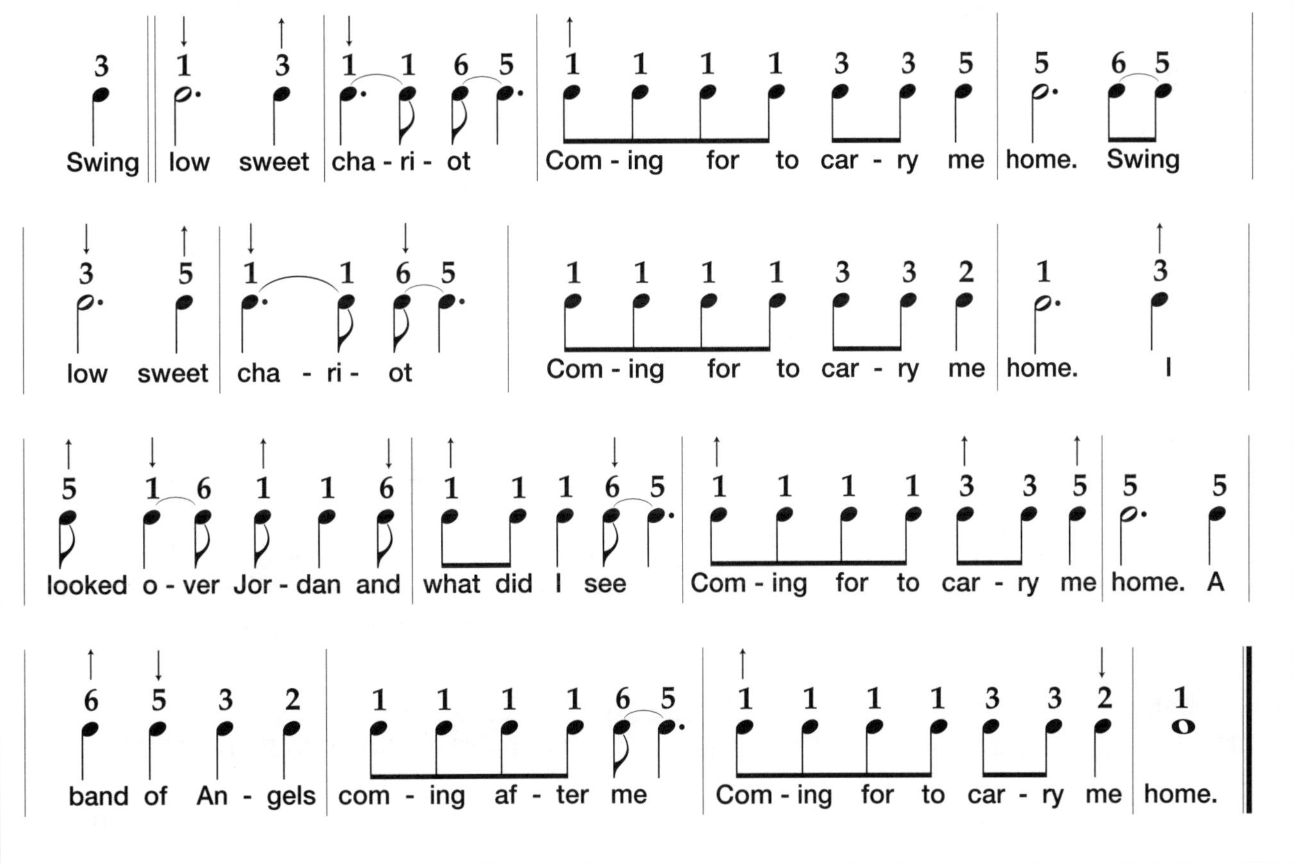

3 | ↓1 ↑3 | ↓1 1 6 5 | ↑1 1 1 1 3 3 5 | 5 6 5 |
Swing | low sweet | cha - ri - ot | Com - ing for to car - ry me | home. Swing |

↓3 ↑5 | ↓1 1 ↓6 5 | 1 1 1 1 3 3 2 | 1 ↑3 |
low sweet | cha - ri - ot | Com - ing for to car - ry me | home. I |

↑5 ↓1 6 ↑1 1 ↓6 | ↑1 1 1 ↓6 5 | ↑1 1 1 1 ↑3 3 ↑5 | 5 5 |
looked o - ver Jor - dan and | what did I see | Com - ing for to car - ry me | home. A |

↑6 ↓5 3 2 | 1 1 1 1 6 5 | ↑1 1 1 1 3 3 ↓2 | 1 ||
band of An - gels | com - ing af - ter me | Com - ing for to car - ry me | home. ||

Presentation

Structure

It is important that your chart be presented in an orderly manner. A song cannot be played effectively if the musician has to spend more effort reading than playing. Chord changes may go fast, and if a player has to take his eyes off a line to search for information, he can get lost very quickly.

There are usually four measures per line, except where phrasing dictates an extra measure. Measures should line up vertically as well as horizontally. Also, enough space should be allowed between measures so that two measures won't be mistaken for a split bar. A split bar should be able to fit in a line and still allow the next measure to align vertically with the above line. So, beforehand, determine the most space you will need between any two measures and leave that much space between every measure.

With a long song, you may run out of room. In this case, you may start a new column on the other side of the page. Some people prefer to write all the way across the page in groups of four measures. If you do so, be sure your musicians know that they should read horizontally before moving down to the next line.

Figure 28

I	....Intro	TA	....Turnaround
V	....Verse	SOLO	....Instrumental Solo
Chnl	....Channel	TAG	....Tag Ending
C	....Chorus		
B	....Bridge		

Symbols such as in Figure 28 should label the beginning of each section, and a line should be drawn under each section to separate it from the next section. Separating sections really helps a player keep his place, and is helpful when discussing sections in a song's arrangement.

I : Intro

The intro is often a short 4 or 8 bar instrumental statement of the melodic hook, or a vamp- to establish the groove and set up the mood of the song.

V : Verse

The verse is the section that describes consequences or tells the story line of a song. There are usually 2 or 3 different verses in a 3 minute song

Chnl : Channel

The channel is sort of a pre-chorus. It's usually the same section of music each time that builds a transition up to the chorus.

[C] : Chorus

The chorus is the section that delivers the musical hook and is usually the basis for the song. The chorus is often repeated after each verse, and a couple of times at the end to reinforce the hook.

[TA] : Turnaround

A turnaround is a short 4 or 8 bar instrumental restatement of the melodic hook. Often, an instrumental version of the last line or two of the chorus will serve as the turnaround.

[B] : Bridge

This is sometimes called the 'middle 8' (if it's 8 bars), and is usually an 8 to 16 bar interlude that will build to the final chorus.

[SOLO] : Solo

A solo is an instrumental section usually over the chords of a verse or a chorus. If you have a certain instrument in mind, write it by the beginning of the [SOLO] section. Example: *Guitar/Steel* [SOLO] : Here the guitar takes the first half of the solo, and the steel plays the second half.

[TAG] : Tag

A tag is usually the last line or two of the final chorus, repeated to signal the end of the song. It sort of puts a cap on the song and is often a repeat of the hook. Be sure to label if a tag is instrumental instead of vocal.

Format

In the upper left hand corner of the chart, write the key, the time signature, the approximate tempo, and a brief description of the feel of the song (Figure 29). Use a metronome marking to give exact tempo.

There should also be any extra information, if necessary, regarding the feel of the song. For example, specific instructions to the bass player like, "walk the bass;" or for the drummer to play "rim clicks during the verse and full snare during the chorus." Often, an example of a standard song with a feel similar to yours may really help pinpoint the idea you are going for.

Figure 29

(G) $\frac{4}{4}$

Medium Fast;

Country Shuffle;

Walk Bass on [C];

Like: *King Of The Road*.

♩ = 100

Arranging

Arranging is a good way to create dynamic excitement in your song's performance. For instance, in the margin, you may assign fills and solos to certain instruments, depending on the band's instrumentation and feel you are trying to capture. When you assign an instrument to "fill" a certain verse or chorus, the instrumentalist will play lines that musically fill spaces between lyrics. For example, you may want to assign the fiddle to split the intro with the steel. Then assign the guitar to fill the verse and steel to fill the chorus; then fiddle plays the turnaround.

You may wish to create dynamics by having the whole band layout, except voice and one other instrument. So, you could instruct, "Band out, solo piano and voice." Then, write, "Band enter" at the point you want them continue playing. *"A cappella"*, on the other hand means all music stops, leaving only voices.

If you write no instructions concerning arrangement, the band will usually add dynamics where they feel. Creative freedom given to your musicians, can lead to some nice arranging that may not have been obvious to you before. Many Nashville musicians prefer a "skeleton" number chart with no information other than the numbers to show chord changes. A "skeleton"chart allows a player freedom to add his own arrangement notes and special instructions for his instrument. Of course if you choose to arrange, there will be no question as to where the musicians will fill and solo. This is where you can eliminate questions and decisions, and save rehearsal or studio time. Check out the arrangement below.

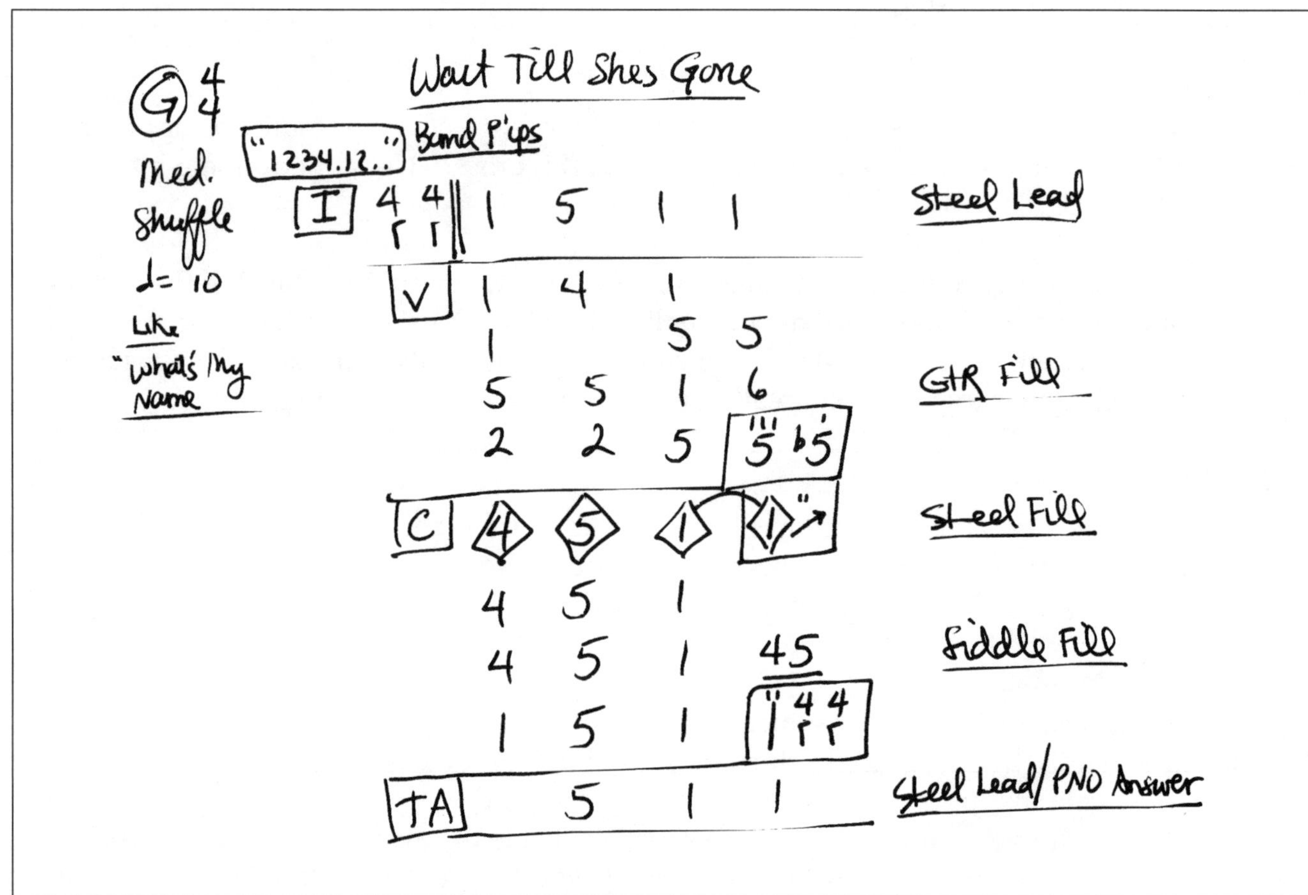

Special Instructions

Tempo

If possible, the exact tempo of a song should be designated with a metronome setting. For example, "♩ = 120 ", means that 4 clicks of a metronome set at 120 will equal one bar of music; also called 120 beats per minute. A musician unfamiliar with a song, and looking at a chart for the first time, may not know whether to read bars with a long, slow count, or *twice* as quickly with a fast count. A song with a halftime feel could be read either way. However, if the player is counting with the wrong tempo, the bars on his chart will be going by either twice as fast or twice as slow as the music is intended. A metronome marking at the top of your chart will eliminate any questions about how the bars are going to be counted.

Count Off

A count off by the drummer, or leader, sets the exact tempo, and allows for any pickup notes to lead into the first measure. A count off is usually two measures, and is counted at the exact tempo with which the song will be played. The proper count off allows a band to begin playing together and to begin playing at the proper tempo. So, if you are counting off your own song, be sure to find the tempo first, then give a 2 measure count at that tempo.

Jimmy Capps sometimes writes the count off that will be given by the drummer. This can be helpful because everyone will know how much of a count to expect, and where the pickup notes begin.

Pickup Notes

Pickup notes are introductory notes that lead into the down beat of the first measure to be played. The pickups are separated from the first measure by a double line. If your song has three quarter note pickups, the drummer would count "1,2,3,4,1..." and the band, or soloist will begin playing the three pickup notes.

Figure 30

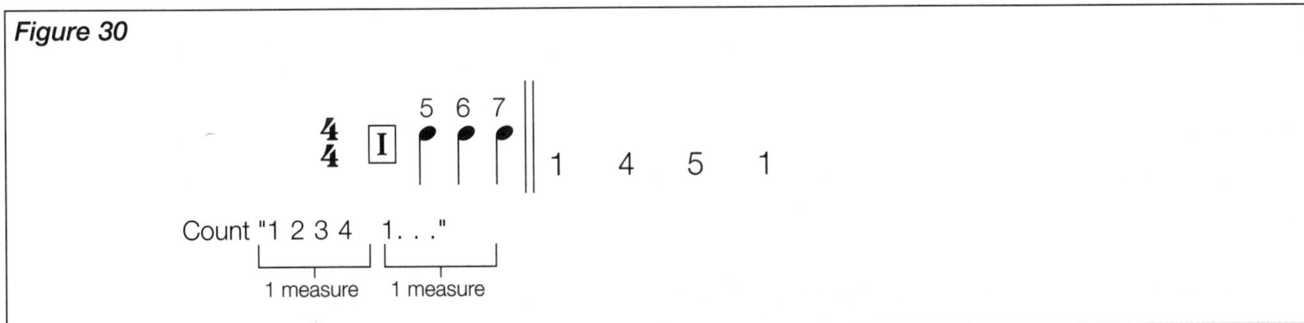

Figure 30 has a two measure count off, and pickups are played on beats "2", "3", & "4" of the second count off measure. Then the first measure of the song begins. Be sure that the pickup notes are not written as part of the first measure. If so, the whole chart will not seem phrased correctly, and may be confusing.

Pickups are usually played by whichever instrument is assigned the lead during the intro. On the other hand, the singer might start the song cold with no instrumental introduction. One example of vocal pickups is *Make The World Go Away*, by Eddy Arnold. Here the vocalist sings for three beats, and the band begins on the second syllable of "away", which is the first down beat of the chorus. So, for the intro of *Make The World Go Away*, write three beats of rest and a memo that there are solo vocal pickups (Figure 31).

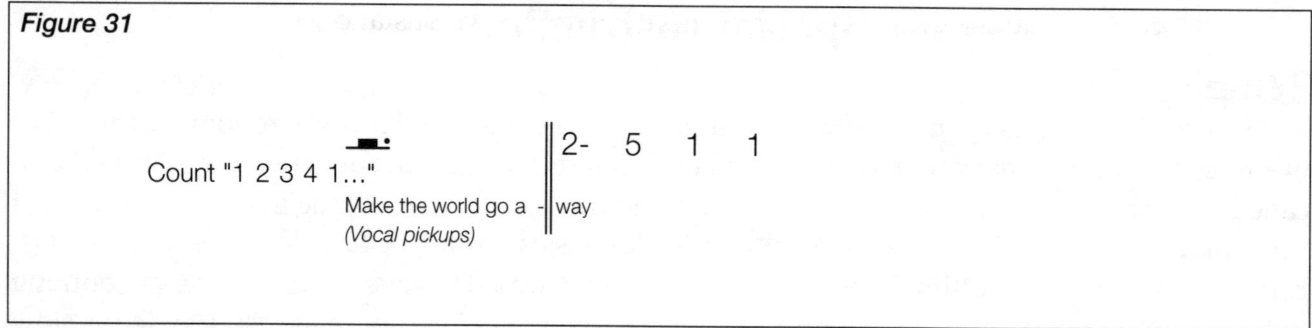

Extra Measure

An extra measure is sometimes added at the end of the line to provide time for an extended vocal phrase or note, or to make room for an instrumental or vocal pickup to the next phrase. We talked extra measures on page 19, under the section called *New Time Signatures*. An extra measure often provides space for a singer to keep phrasing even. There may be more than one extra measure, but they are written to the right of the measure whose phrase they extend. The important idea is to have the beginning of a musical or vocal phrase start at the beginning of a new line. The song *Daddy's Hands*, by Holly Dunn counted in cut time, has an extra measure at the end of the 2nd and 3rd lines of the chorus. Figure 32 is the chorus of *Daddy's Hands*. Notice the extra measures at the end of the 2nd and 3rd lines instead of at the beginning of the lines that follow.

Figure 32

¢	C	2	1	4	1	
		3-	6-	4	5	5
		1	1	4	2	2
		1 4	1 5	1	1	

Repeat Signs 𝄆 𝄇

Play from one repeat sign to the other, return to the first and repeat everything within the signs. Then, move on to the next section.

For example, if a verse is played twice in a row, but has a slightly different ending the second time, you may use repeat signs and write a first and second ending. In Figure 33, play through the 1st ending. Take the repeat and play the section again. The second time, skip the 1st ending, play the 2nd ending and go on to the next section.

Figure 33

𝄆 1	4	5	1			
1	4	5	1			
1	4	5	1			
6-	2-	1. 4	5 𝄇	2. 4	1^7	

If the section included needs repeating more than once for instance, write 3x's by the last repeat sign, like in Figure 34.

Figure 34

𝄆	1	4	5	1	
	1	4	5	1	
	1	4	5	1	
	1	4	5	1 𝄇	3x's

It's usually best to write out an entire section rather than try to save space by repeating lines within a section. In other words, you wouldn't write the Verse, in Figure 35 below, with repeats around the 1st line and instructions to repeat those 4 bars 3x's. You write out the entire verse.

D.S. al 𝄌

D.S. is an abbreviation of the latin instruction to return to the sign (𝄋). ***Al*** **𝄌**, means play to the Coda (𝄌). ***D.S. al*** 𝄌 could be used as a short cut if there is a difference between two sections, so you won't have to write out the whole section again.

Figure 35

	I	1	5	1	1
𝄋	V	1	4	5	1
		1	4	5	1
		1	4	5	1
		6-	2-	5	1
	C	4	4	1	1
		4	4	1	1
		4	4	1	1 𝄌
		5	5	5	5 *D.S. al* 𝄌
𝄌		5	5	5	1 5 1 𝄐

In Figure 35, play the first verse and chorus until it says ***D.S. al*** 𝄌. We return to the sign 𝄋 and play the verse a second time to the coda 𝄌. Then, we jump to the other coda 𝄌, skipping the last line of the second chorus and instead, playing the Coda line. ***D.C. al*** 𝄌 is the same as ***D.S. al*** 𝄌, except ***D.C.*** means return to the very beginning of the song, instead of the 𝄋 then play to the coda, 𝄌.

Please consider though, that short cuts can be confusing. With a ***D.S. al*** 𝄌, the player has to take his eyes off the chart to find the 𝄋 then again to search for the new 𝄌. If in doubt, sometimes it is safer to write out the entire section rather than save a little ink on a short cut.

Vamp

Sometimes, for an intro, recitation section of a song, or fade, you may want the band to fall into a holding pattern over a certain progression. This is called a vamp. The band vamps over the section which is enclosed with repeat signs until the leader cues to move on to the next section.

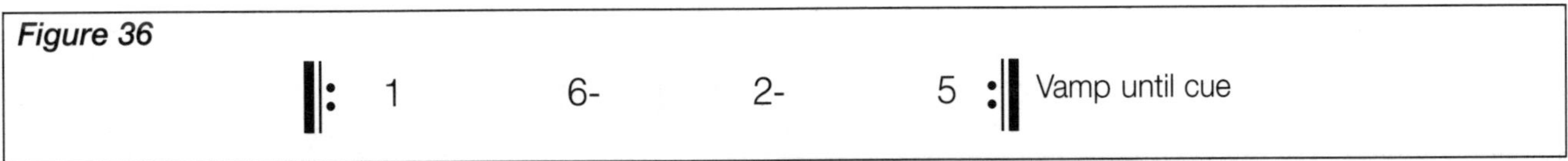

Modulation

A modulation is when you change keys during a song. There are many ways to modulate. One of the more common ways is to go straight to the new key. After the last bar in the original key, write ***Mod*** ↗, and the amount of steps involved, or the chord of the song to which you're modulating, and encircle the new key. Immediately after the modulation sign, (***Mod*** ↗), the chord numbers will not change, but they will be read as in the new key. In Figure 37, the first line ends with a **C** chord, or ***1***, in the key of **C**. The first chord which appears after the modulation is now a **D**, or ***1*** in the key of **D**.

Figure 37

Key of (C)	1	4	5	1	***Mod*** ↗ 1 step (D)
Key of (D)	1	4	5	1	

Another type of modulation is to use the ***5*** chord of the new key, or the "New ***5***", and then write modulation instructions.

Figure 38

Key of (C)	1	4	5	6^7 (new 5)***Mod*** ↗ 1 step (D)	
Key of (D)	1	4	5	1	

In Figure 38, the 6^7 is the 5^7 of the new key, but is written as the 6^7 in the original key.

If you wanted to modulate only a half step use **#5** as the new ***5***. In Figure 39, **#**5^7 will be the ***5*** of the new key of **C#**, a half step above the original key of **C**.

Figure 39

Key of (C)	1	4	5	#5^7 (new 5)***Mod*** ↗ 1/2 step (C#)	
Key of (C#)	1	4	5	1	

Look at Figure 40. We're modulating more than a step; C up to E*b*. You can say," Mod ↗ to ***b3***", which is ***b3*** of the old key (C), but becomes ***1*** of the new key(E*b*). So, in Figure 40, the 1st chord after the modulation is ***4*** in the key of E*b*, or an A*b*.

Figure 40

Key of (C)	1	4	5	1	*Mod* ↗ *to "b3"* (E*b*)
Key of (E*b*)	4	5	1	1	

Walkups and Walkdowns

Sometimes, when you have a basic scalar walkup or walkdown from one chord to the next, you may abbreviate the notation with an arrow pointing in the direction of the target chord.

Figure 41

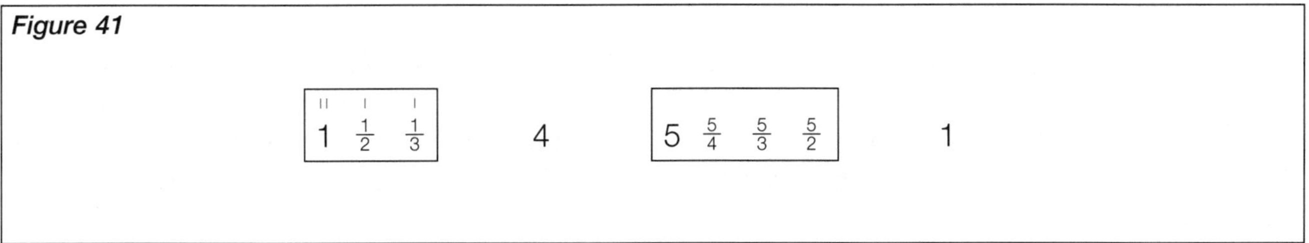

The above line can be written as in Figure 41.

Figure 42

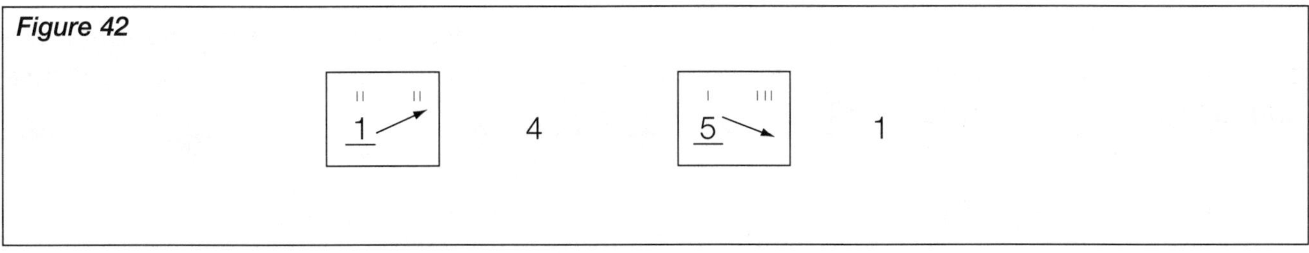

Remember though, the arrow is simple shorthand and will work only in place of a quarter note, major scale approach to the new chord. Notice how measure 1 in Figure 40 is shown as a split bar and the *1* chord gets 2 beats. Therefore, the arrow can represent only a 2 beat walkup. As follows, the *5* chord in the third measure gets one beat allowing time for a three beat walkdown.

Dynamics

There are several signs which tell a player how to attack a note, or perhaps how not to attack it. There are signs for loudness, sustain, anticipation, speed, punch, and other ways of playing a note or chord. These different approaches to a certain note or phrase are called dynamics. Dynamic indicators can really help communicate the kind of feeling and personality you want translated into the music.

Diamond ◇

A diamond means to strike the chord and let it ring for its designated duration. Simply draw a diamond around the chord to be held. Below, the final bar, called a *"One diamond"*, is struck and held for one full measure, or 4 beats.

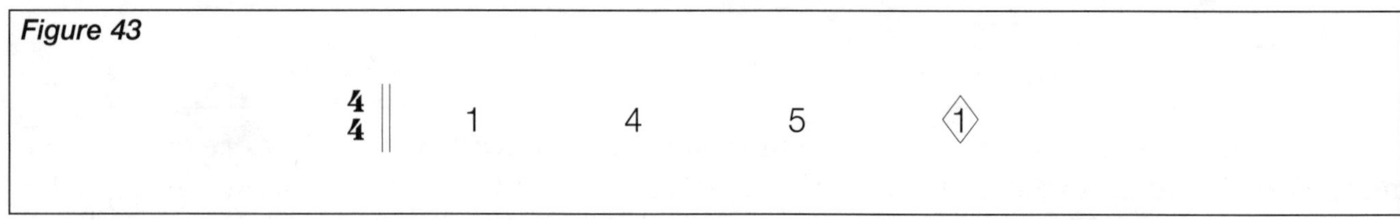

Some people write small diamonds above or below the chord, as in Figure 44.

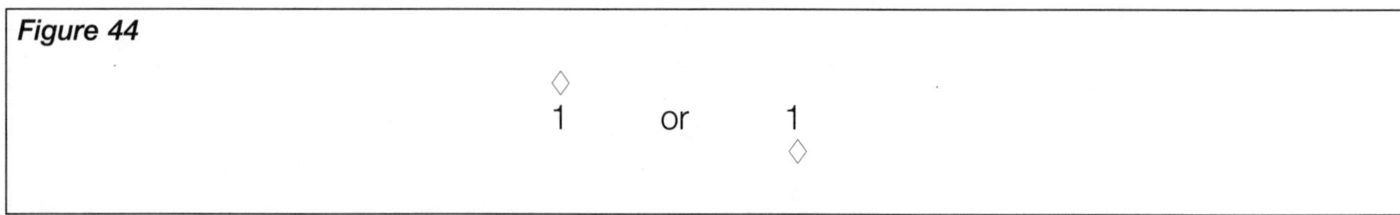

A tied diamond shows that the chord is held for the extra duration notated. In Figure 45, the 5 chord in the third measure is struck and held for its measure plus the next measure, or a total of eight beats.

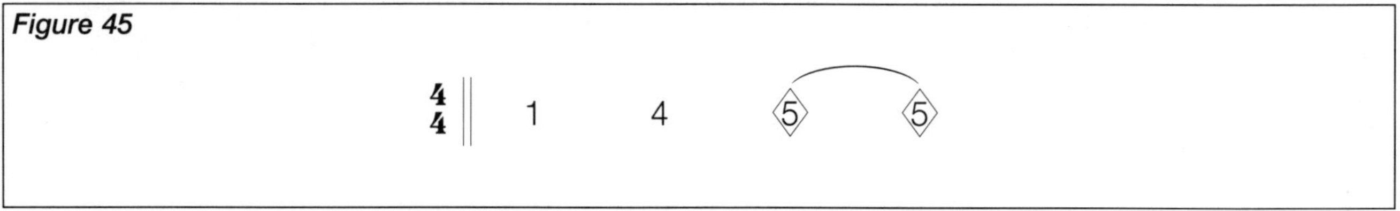

Bird's Eye or Fermata 𝄐

The bird's eye is a symbol taken from formal notation. When placed over the chord, it means the chord is struck and held until there is a cue from whoever is conducting the band. For example, in the tag of *Forever and Ever Amen*, by Randy Travis, the band hits the $\overset{\frown}{5}$ chord and holds it while Randy sings, "Amen." There is no countable way for the band to come back in together, so they must rely on a hand signal, or cue from whoever is conducting the ending.

Cut Off or Mute

A ▲ or • above the chord means that the chord is struck and muted, or cut off. You don't allow the chord to ring for the full beat. Here, the *1* (with ▲ above) is struck and muted, though the full measure is counted.

Figure 46

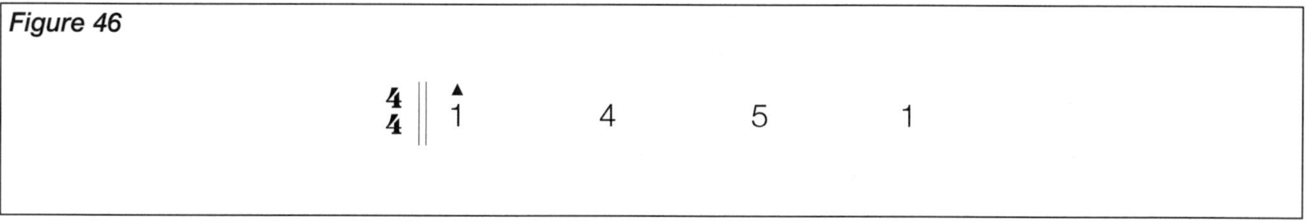

In Figure 47, there is a bar with two muted attacks on the *1* chord plus a 2 beat rest.

Figure 47

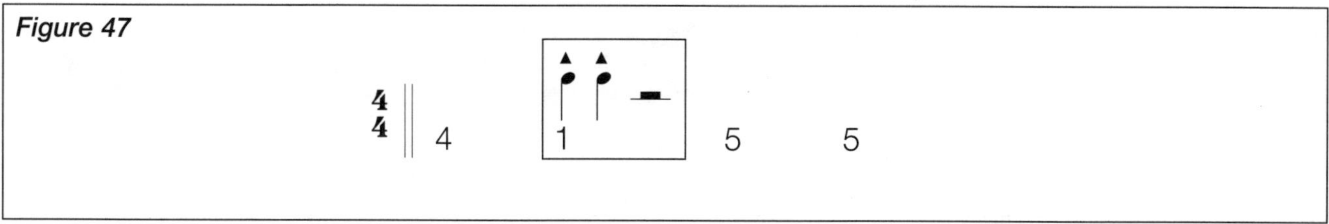

Anticipation >

Below, the **6-** is struck on the "and" or upbeat of beat 2 of the measure.

Figure 48

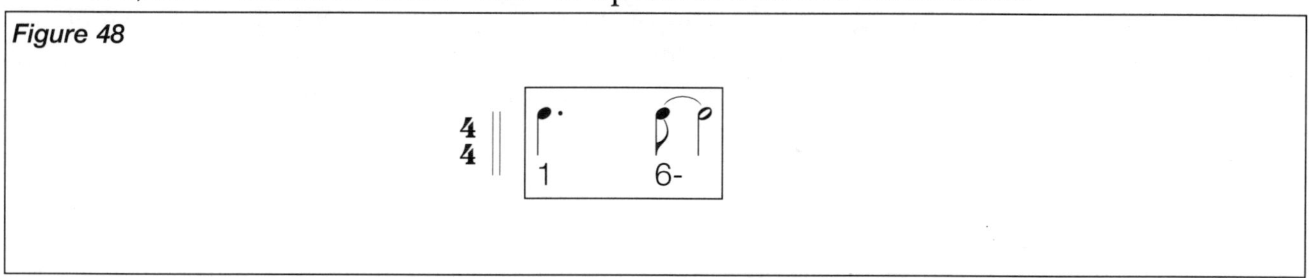

A small horizontal arrow over a chord can also mean that the chord is anticipated or pushed. Figure 49 is a fast, easy way to write Figure 48, using the push sign. It is true, this arrow is a dynamics symbol borrowed from traditional notation.

Figure 49

4/4 ‖ 1 6- (with > above the 6-)

Loudness

The loudness sign is written beneath a passage or phrase. When pointing to the right, it means to begin reducing the volume at the open end, and be the quietest at the tip of the sign. On the contrary, when the loudness sign points to the left, it means to begin increasing in volume at the closed point, and be the loudest where the sign is open. These symbols are good for writing in a big crescendo, or setting up a really quiet passage for dynamic contrast.

In Figure 50, begin volume increase at the second measure and be loudest at the fourth measure.

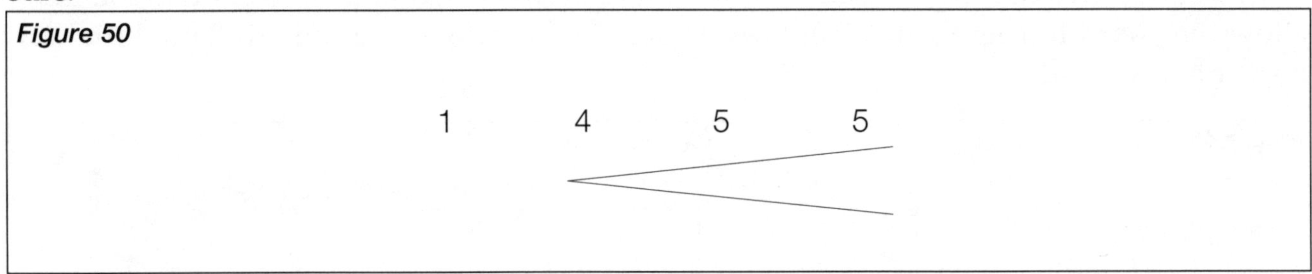

Figure 50

In Figure 51, begin volume decrease at the second measure and be the quietest at the fourth measure.

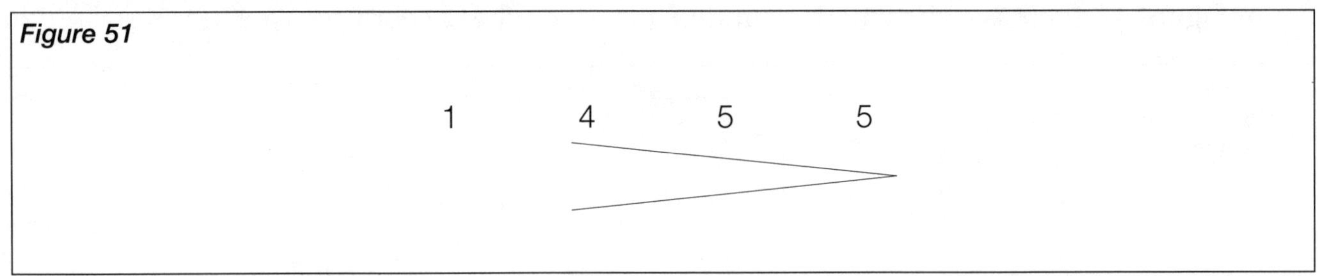

Figure 51

Ritard *rit.* ——————

The ritard sign under a section means to gradually slow down tempo. Begin slowing at the *Ritard* sign and continue slowing until the end of the sign. *Ritards* are effective for dramatically bringing the dynamics down to a quieter level or ending a song. However, if you want to *ritard* during the song and then return to the original tempo, write *"a tempo"* where the original tempo should resume.

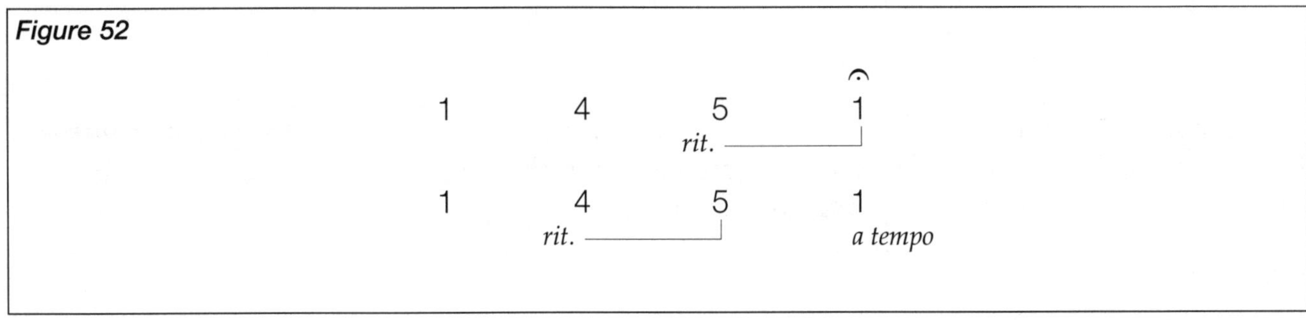

Figure 52

Feel and Style

Feel and Style

Possibly the most important information to convey to musicians is the proper feel of your song. Here, language is essential, because there are many ways for a musician to interpret a particular style. It is necessary to accurately describe the kind of rythmic feel you want. For example, there are many variations of the halftime feel. When you ask for a Don Williams halftime, a drummer will usually use a cross stick on the 2 and 4 beats, and play a pattern of sixteenth notes on the snare and hi-hat with brushes.

It is a good idea to talk to the musicians around town, especially drummers, and learn what they call different musical techniques and styles. If there is a situation where you have a variation of a standard feel, you will need to know what techniques to ask of the drummer.

For example, *cross stick* is the correct term for the sound when a drummer holds a stick sideways and clicks it on the rim of the snare. However, many people call this technique a "rimshot." Actually, a rimshot is a hard hit on the snare close to the rim, for dynamically loud sections. Eddie Bayers makes a good point, however. He said that it would be nice if everyone used correct terms for drumming techniques, but if the person who hired you is calling cross sticking a rimshot, then that's what it's called.

There are so many sounds available to musicians these days, it can only help to learn some of the language that will accurately describe what you are hearing for your song.

$\frac{4}{4}$ Common Time

A majority of popular music on the radio these days is written in some form of $\frac{4}{4}$, or common time. In formal music notation, the symbol **C**, stands for Common Time.

Of course, there are many ways to play 4 quarter notes per measure. The following feel descriptions may be helpful ways to talk about a particular groove you may have in mind for your song.

Swing

This describes a groove with a real bounce or lilt. Instead of a straight eighth note feel: , you have more of a triplet feel: . The first 2 bars of the melody for *In the Mood*, by Duke Ellington, would be written like Figure 53.

Figure 53

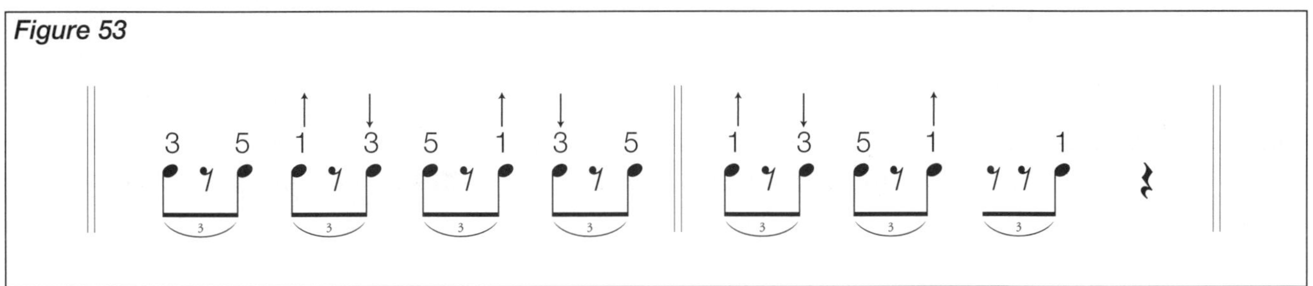

Texas swing has a feel of its own. Generally, when you say Texas swing it implies a $\frac{2}{4}$ feel on drums with a 2 beat bass. On a *2 beat swing*, the bass mostly plays notes ***1*** and ***5*** of the chord at beats 1 and 3 of each measure. The rhythm guitar usually plays the rhythm pattern: $\frac{4}{4}$ 𝄽 ♩ 𝄽 ♩ | 𝄽 ♩ 𝄽 ♩ ‖, with accents on the upbeats. Of course, there are many varieties of Texas Swing. The Bob Wills song, *Deep Water* has a 2 beat feel on the verses and *walks* (plays quarter notes through the chord changes) on the choruses. *San Antonio Rose* would have a swinging two-four feel with the bass playing the ***root*** and 5 of each chord change. You would call this a *2 beat swing* since the bass and bass drum are emphasizing beats 1 and 3 of each measure instead of walking. Listen to some Asleep At The Wheel records for good examples of Texas Swing.

Shuffle

This describes a type of swing that isn't quite as exaggerated as the Texas Swing. There are many types of shuffles. *On the Other Hand*, by Randy Travis, is a medium slow country shuffle. It is a 2 beat shuffle with the bass playing on the beats 1 and 3 of each measure.

Ray Price developed such a style of shuffle, that the "Ray Price Shuffle" implies a walking bass and a jazzy, behind the beat feel. *Born To Lose* is an excellent example of a "Ray Price Shuffle." Often on a Price Shuffle, the band will play some version of Figure 54.

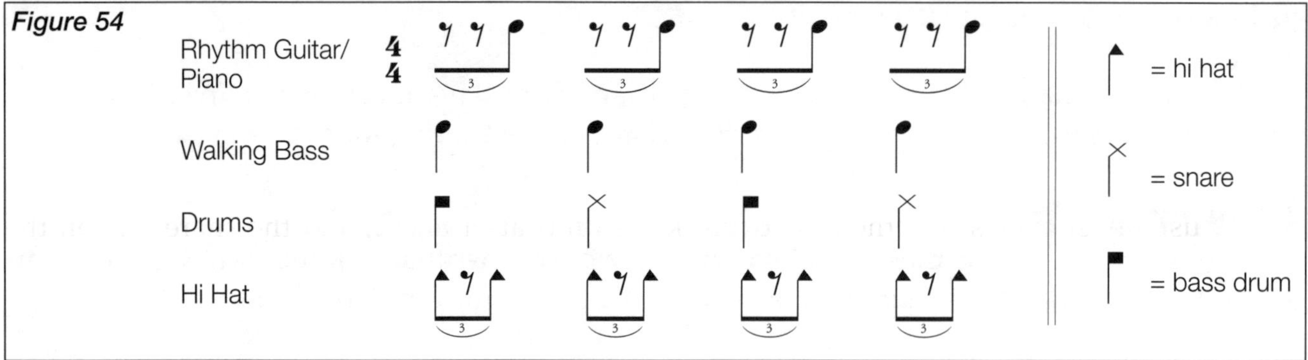

Rock

When you use the term "Rock," a drummer usually will play the pattern in Figure 55:

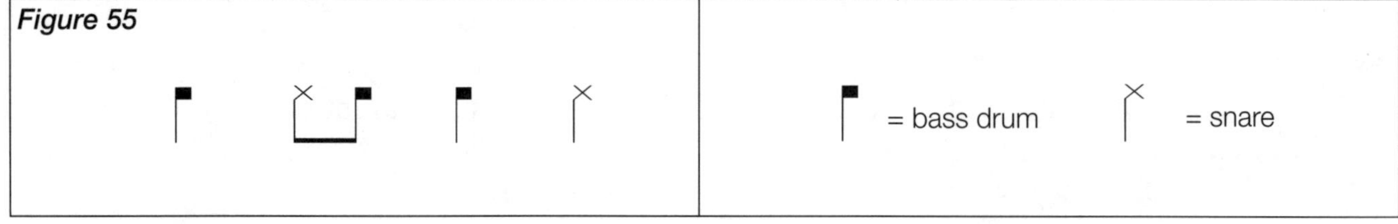

The pattern the drummer plays on his hi-hat or ride cymbal will often define whether the song has a shuffle or a straight feel.

Rock Shuffle

Memphis and *Guitar Boogie* are examples of a country rock shuffle. The song *Rosanna*, by Toto is a heavier rock shuffle, with a halftime feel. Another good example of a rock shuffle would be *Born to Boogie*, by Hank Williams, Jr. *Kansas City* is more of a *blues shuffle*. It helps to have an idea what kind of shuffle you're asking for, and if possible, to have a couple of song titles that have a similar feel what you're wanting to describe.

Straight Feel or "Eighths"

A straight feel implies a rigid, straight quarter or eighth note feel. The term "Eighths" usually means a straight eighth note pattern on the hi-hat and rhythm instruments. Some examples of "straight eighths" are: *Tequila Sunrise,* by the Eagles and *Swinging,* by John Anderson. *He Stopped Loving Her Today,* by George Jones could be called an "Eighths Ballad".

Rock Eighths

Rock eighths also implies a straight eighths rhythmic feel. Songs such as *Wipe Out,* by The Safaris and *Heart of Rock and Roll,* by Huey Lewis would be described as rock eighths. Also, *Achy Breaky Heart,* by Billy Ray Cyrus, and *Pink Cadillac,* by Bruce Springsteen have a straight eighths feel.

Two Four $\frac{2}{4}$

$\frac{2}{4}$ is often used when charting a faster 2 beat feel. This time signature is counted "1 and 2 and, 1 and 2 and."

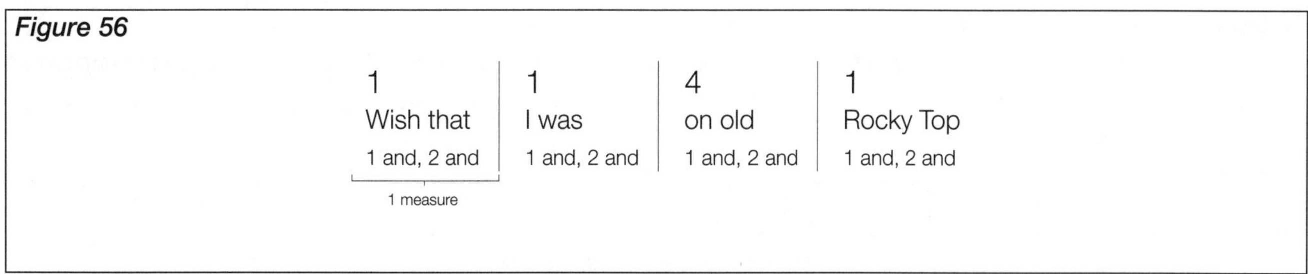

$\frac{2}{4}$ usually suggests that the bass drum kicks on beats 1 and 2, and the snare hits on the "and," or upbeats. Many times a song with a $\frac{2}{4}$ or ¢ feel will have the drummer use a *"train beat"* like in Figure 57 below. The drummer is playing sixteenth notes on the snare, but still accents the upbeats.

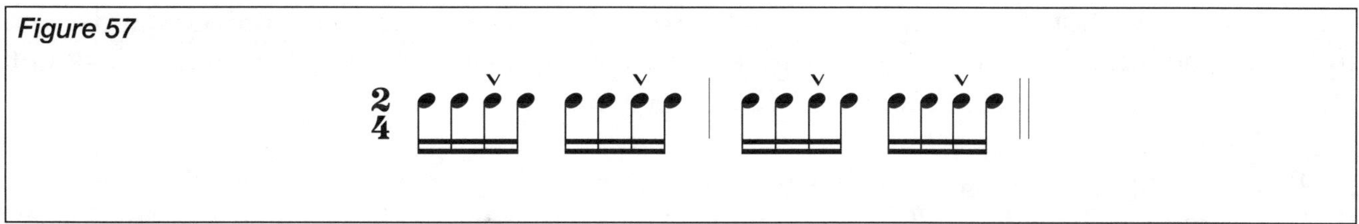

Cut Time

In cut time, you divide a $\frac{4}{4}$ bar in half. The bar is read as $\frac{2}{2}$. A half note gets one beat; 2 halfnotes per bar. So, eighth notes from the same $\frac{4}{4}$ piece are written and counted as quarter notes. As well, sixteenth notes are written as eighth notes and rhythmic notation is easier all around. One measure of regular time equals two measures of cut time.

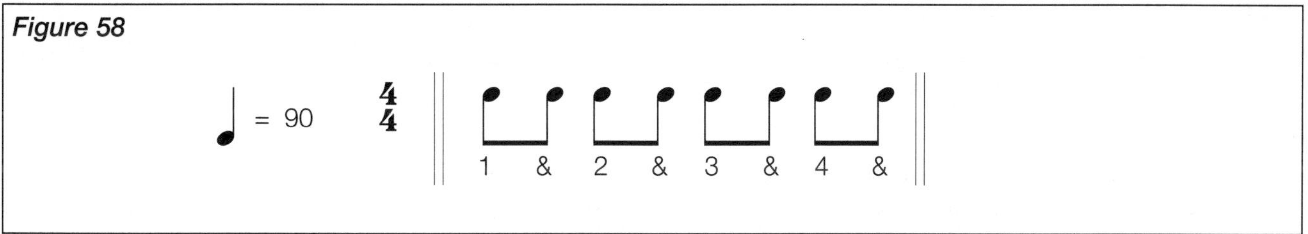

Figure 58 written in cut time will look like Figure 59.

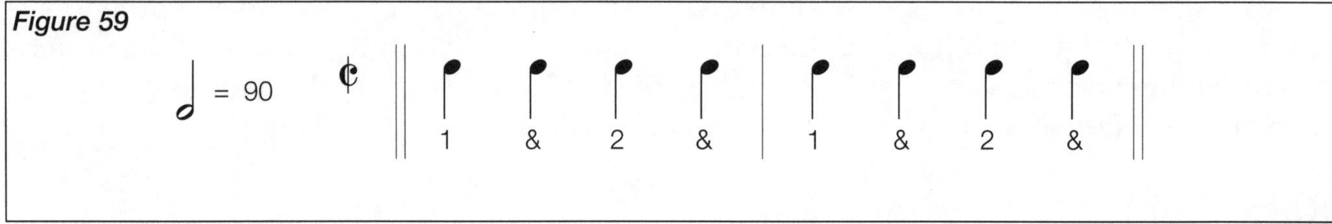

Cut time generally implies a song with a brisker pace and a 2 beat feel. Like $\frac{2}{4}$, it is also counted,"One and Two and." Most often, for a song with a halftime feel, you may write the chart in cut time.

Halftime Feel

Halftime implies a more elongated approach to the feel of a song. Instead of the snare drum, or backbeat falling on the "and" or upbeat of every measure, it falls on beats 2 and 4 of every measure. So, the time feels expanded, or longer and slower; though the actual tempo doesn't change.

Are You Sure Hank Done It This Way, by Waylon Jennings has a halftime feel. The bass guitar and bass drum hit on beats 1 2 3 & 4 and the snare on beats 2 & 4.

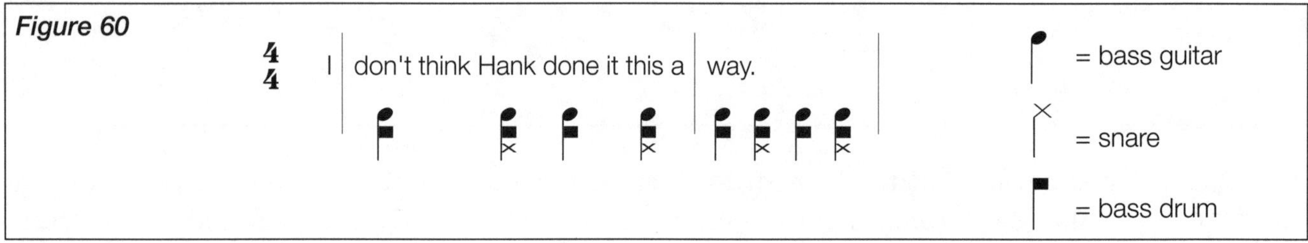

If you wanted to change from a halftime feel to a $\frac{2}{4}$ feel for the chorus, you would write " $\frac{2}{4}$ feel" by the chorus section. The drummer would then hit the snare on the "ands," or upbeats. The added backbeats would give the song the faster $\frac{2}{4}$ feel. The tempo does not change, but there are twice as many backbeats per measure.

Richie Albright, who played drums on Waylon Jenning's records in the early '70's, was the first to introduce the halftime feel into country music. Richie says he listened to "The Band" alot, and translated some of the feels they were getting into Waylon's sound. Richie developed his own version of a halftime feel and first used it on *Lonesome, Ornery, and Mean*, then other Waylon hits around 1972 and 1973. Since, the halftime feel has become a standard approach to many country songs, and has evolved into many variations.

I'm A Ramblin' Man, by Waylon Jennings has a halftime feel. However, if the chart is written in regular time, the bass guitar and bass drum would note on every beat of the measure; beats 1, 2, 3 and 4. The snare, or backbeat would hit on downbeats 2 and 4 of each measure, instead of the "and" of each beat, thus giving the song the slower, halftime feel.

If you notated the 1st measure of the *I'm A Ramblin' Man* intro guitar lick in regular time, it would look like Figure 61.

Figure 61

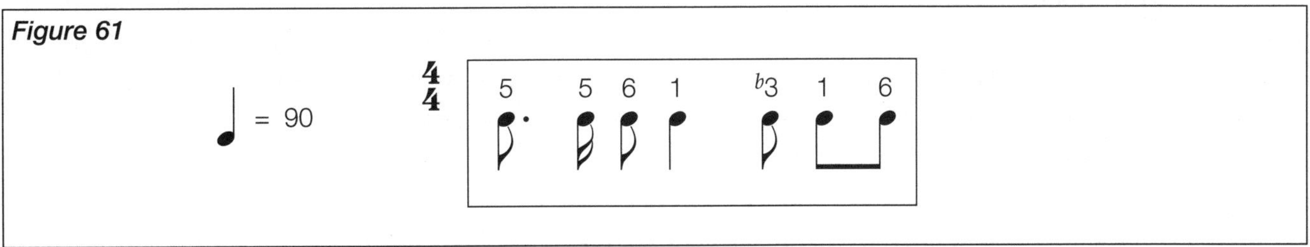

So, we can write the chart in cut time instead. The halftime feel remains because everything is played the same, but it's alot easier to subdivide a halfnote at 90 bpm than a quarter note. As a result, the same intro guitar lick on *I'm A Ramblin' Man*, would be written in cut time as two measures, like in Figure 62.

Figure 62

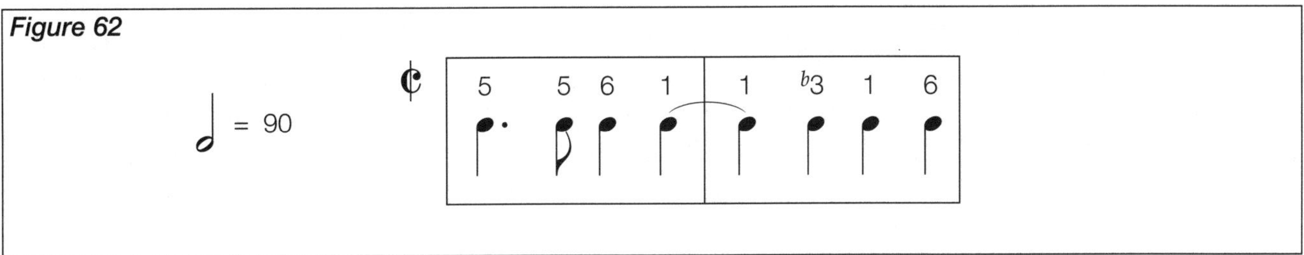

To describe the feel of *I'm A Ramblin' Man*, write Figure 63:

Figure 63

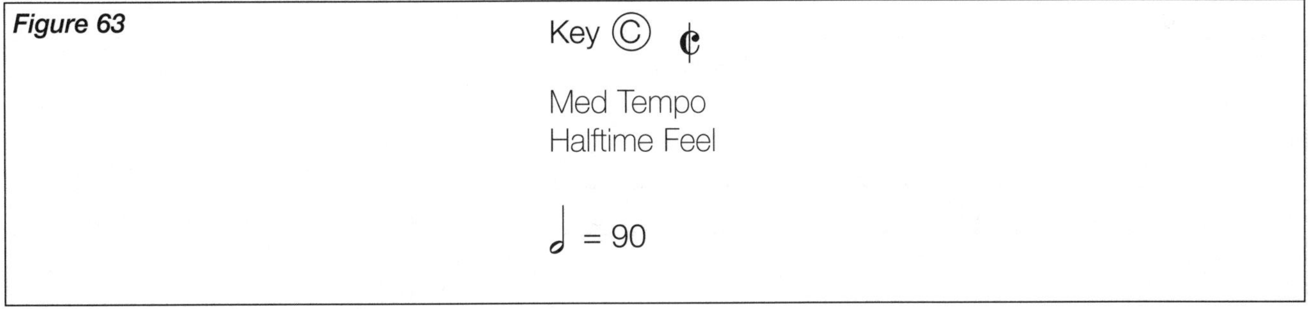

$\frac{3}{4}$ Waltz

$\frac{3}{4}$ or Waltz is a song counted with three beats per measure. *Rose Colored Glasses*, by John Conlee, *Tennessee Waltz*, by Pee Wee King, and *Waltz Across Texas*, by Ernest Tubb all have the basic waltz feel of counting in "3".

$\frac{6}{8}$ Halftime Waltz

It's hard to decide whether to use $\frac{3}{4}$ or $\frac{6}{8}$. $\frac{6}{8}$ generally implies more of a half time waltz, or a Waylon Jennings feel. In *the* $\frac{6}{8}$ tune, *Mamas Don't Let Your Babies Grow Up To Be Cowboys*, by Waylon, the bass drum kicks on beat 1, and the snare hits on beat 4, while the hi-hat plays eighths. The result is the elongated half time feel shown in Figure 64.

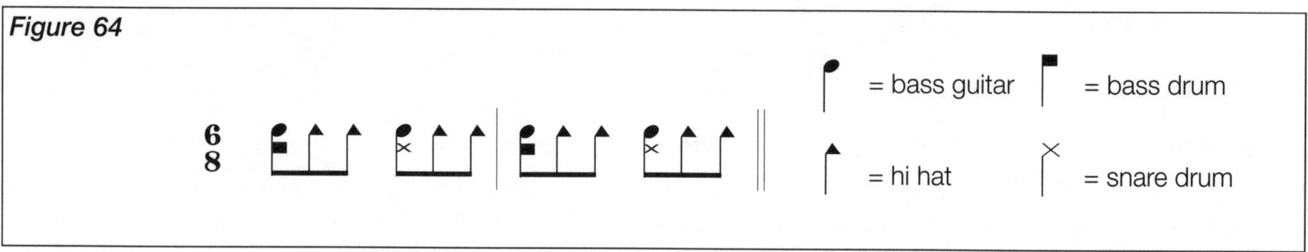

Ballad

When you say "ballad", you imply a more serious mood and probably a slow or medium slow eighths feel. Ballads are generally more dramatic pieces of music, like, *Wind Beneath My Wings,* by Bette Midler, or *My Way*, by Elvis. You can also have a ballad that swings with a triplet feel. *You Gave Me A Mountain*, also by Elvis is a ballad with triplet feel. It feels like a slow 4 until the end, where it reallypounds out the triplets.

Triplet Feel

Figure 65 could be described as $\frac{12}{8}$,or a slower $\frac{4}{4}$. The hi-hat and rhythm guitars might play a triplet figure, while the bass and bass drum thump out beats 1 and 3. The snare would hit on beats 2 and 4.

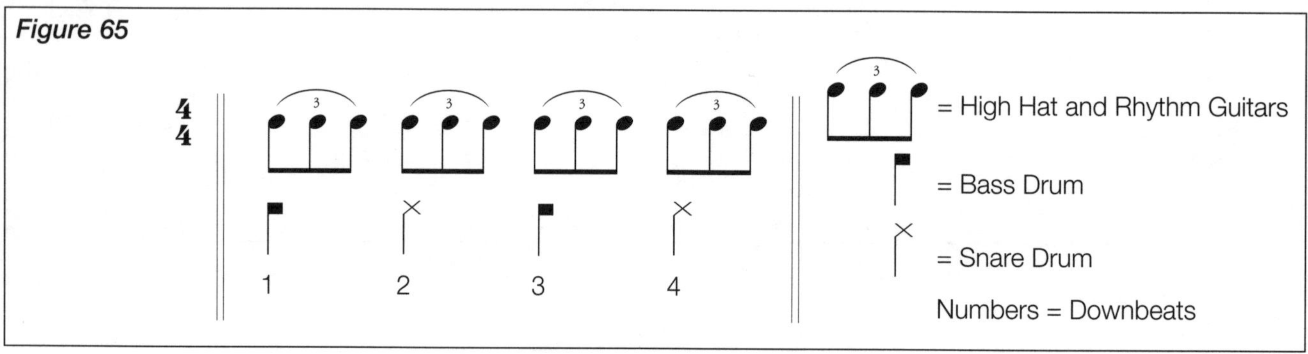

This is called a polyrhythm. Within the rhythm section, there are two or more separate rhythmic figures working together to create the unique triplet feel.

Some other songs that have a triplet feel are: *Blueberry Hill*, by Fats Domino, *Unchained Melody*, by The Righteous Brothers, and *Statue Of A Fool*, by Jack Greene. Use a triplet feel for a slow ballad if you want it to have a bit of a swing.

Handwritten Charts

This section includes charts handwritten from 7 classic country standards. The charts are taken from the original hit singles: *Crazy Arms*, by Ray Price; *Heartbreak Hotel*, by Elvis Presley; *Rocky Top*, by The Osborne Brothers; *Last Cheaters Waltz*, by T.G. Shepard; *Mammas Don't Let Your Babies Grow Up To Be Cowboys*, by Waylon Jennings and Willie Nelson; *Crazy*, by Patsy Cline; and *Funny How Time Slips Away*, by Ray Price; also, *He Stopped Loving Her Today*, by George Jones.

Each chart is handwritten by some of Nashville's most influential and prestigious musicians, including: Charlie McCoy (*Hee Haw*), Jimmy Capps (*Grand Ole Opry*), Lura Foster (*Prime Time Country/Music City Tonight/Nashville Now*), Barry Beckett (*Nashville/Muscle Shoals producer and studio keyboardist*), Eddie Bayers (*studio drummer*), and Brent Mason (*One of Nashville's first call studio guitarists*).

This combination of charts shows the different styles and types of notations that you may run across in the recording and television studios, as well as almost any end of the performance side of the music business in Nashville.

Charlie McCoy

Charlie studied music at the University of Miami. He moved to Nashville and began working recording sessions in the early '60's. After playing on Roy Orbison's hit, *Candy Man*, Charlie built up to more than 400 sessions a year. In addition to sessions with country artists, Charlie has played on many of Elvis Presley's records, as well as three albums for Bob Dylan. Charlie has had quite a recording career of his own, with 12 albums on the *Monument* label. (For information on how to order Charlie's records, write: Charlie McCoy, 116 17th Ave. So., Nashville, TN 37203).

In the early '60's, Charlie, Wayne Moss, and David Briggs, noticed how Neal Matthews, and *The Jordanaires* were using numbers to map out a song chart. Charlie, David, and Wayne began figuring how to use numbers for chord charts, and were the first to initiate use of the *Nashville Number System* for the instrumentalist on sessions.

Charlie played harmonica and served as the musical director for the Hee Haw television show for 18 years. He arranged and wrote all the charts that the band read.

Charlie writes his charts horizontally across the page in groups of four measures. He draws a box around split bars and writes diamonds beneath the chord number. For rhythmic notation like on *Heartbreak Hotel*, Charlie writes the rhythms beneath the chord changes. These charts are very clear and easy to follow. There is never a question as to what chord and section is coming up next.

Fayetteville, West Virginia probably never realized that Charlie McCoy was going to become such an innovator and deciding factor in the way country music was going to be notated and recorded. A veteran player on thousands of record sessions, Charlie has been primary in developing the standard for how music will be written in Nashville for years to come.

Rightly so, the *Nashville Number System* is gradually spreading to the different recording centers of the world. Thanks to Neal Matthews and The Jordanaires, Charlie McCoy, Wayne Moss, David Briggs, and all the other musicians who have added to the development of the *Nashville Number System*.

Crazy Arms

Fiddle 1 5 1 1

V) 1 1 4 1   1 1 5 5   1 1 4 1   1 5 1 1

C) 1 1 4 1   1 1 5 5   1 1 4 1   1 5 1 1 2x.

Steel solo 1 5 1 1

Charlie McCoy

Heartbreak Hotel

4x's

Vocal pick ups | 1 | 1 | Bass lead 1 | 4 4 5 1

Inst Elec 1 1 1 1 Pno 4 4 5 1

1 | 1 | | | 4 4 5 1

1

1

Charlie McCoy

Rocky Top

1 1 4 1 6m 5 1 1

V1
V3 [1 1 4 1 6m 5 1 1 1 1 4 1 6m 5 1 1

V2
V4 1 1 4 1 6m 5 1 1 1 1 4 1 6m 5 1 1

6m 6m 5 5 7b 7b 4 4 4 4 1 1 1 7b 1

1 7b 1 1]

INST 1 1 4 1 6m 5 1 1 1 1 4 1 6m 5 1 1

6m 6m 5 5 7b 7b 4 4 4 4 1 1 1 7b 1 1

7b 1 1

V5 1 1 4 1 6m 5 1 1 1 1 4 1 6m 5 1 1

6m 6m 5 5 7b 7b 4 4 4 4 1 1 1 7b 1 1

1 7b 1 1 1 7b 7 1 1 7b 7b 4 4 1 1 1 1

PIP

LAST CHEATER'S WALTZ

3/4 1 1△/△ 6m | 5/1 6m/1 5/7 |

V1 1111 4444 5555 55 1 | 5 6m 5/7 |

V2 1111 4444 5555 55 1 | 5 6m 5/7 |

CHO 1 5/7 6m 1/5 4 4⁶ 4△ 4⁶ 5 2m 5 5 1 | 5 6m 5/7 |

1 5/7 6m 1/5 4 4⁶ 4△ 4⁶ 5 2m 5 5 1 | 5 6m 5/7 |

INST 1111 1155 2m 2m△/2b 2m/1 5/7 55 1 | 5 6m 5/7 |

CHO 1 5/7 6m 1/5 4 4⁶ 4△ 4⁶ 5 2m 5 5 1 | 5 6m 5/7 |

RIT

1 5/7 6m 1/5 4 4⁶ 4△ 4⁶ 5 2m 5 5 1 | 5 6m 5/7 |

1 (fermata)

[signature]

MAMA DON'T LET YOUR BABIES

3/4 1111

V1 1111 4444 5555 1111

1111 4444 5555 5511-11

CHO 1111 4444 5555 5551-1

1111 4444 5555 5511-11 MOD 1 STEP

V2 1111 4444 5555 1111

1111 4444 5555 5511-11

FADE

CHO [1111 4444 5555 5551-1

1111 4444 5555 5511-11]

CRAZY

1 4 | 4 3m | 2m 5 |

(V) 1 6 2m 2m 5 | 5 5+ | 1 1#° | 2m 5 |

1 6 2m 2m 5 5 | 1 2m | 3♭° $\frac{1^7}{3}$ |

4 | 4 4#° | 1 | 1 7 1 1# | 2 2 5 5

1 6 2m 2m | 4 3m | 2m $\frac{6}{1\#}$ | 2m 5 | 1 5# | MOD ½

1 6 2m 2m | 4 3m | 2m $\frac{6}{1\#}$ | 2m 5

1 4 1

Funny How Time Slips Away

1 1 1 1

V1 V2 [14 1 1 1411 1 1^{7}4 2 5 [2m5] [14] [15]

TA 5 5 1 1

V3 1411 1411 1 1^{7}4 2 5 [2m5] [14]

Jimmy Capps

Jimmy moved to Nashville in 1958, while working with the Louvin Brothers. He played on the *Grand Ole Opry* for the first time in 1962. In 1968, Jimmy became a full time guitarist for the Opry staff band, and has played Friday and Saturday nights there since.

As well, Jimmy has played on alot of great records. A few of the classic songs that he played guitar on are *Stand By Your Man*, by Tammy Wynette, *Easy Lovin*, by Freddy Hart, *The Gambler* and *Coward Of The County*, by Kenny Rogers, and *Elvira*, by the Oak Ridge Boys.

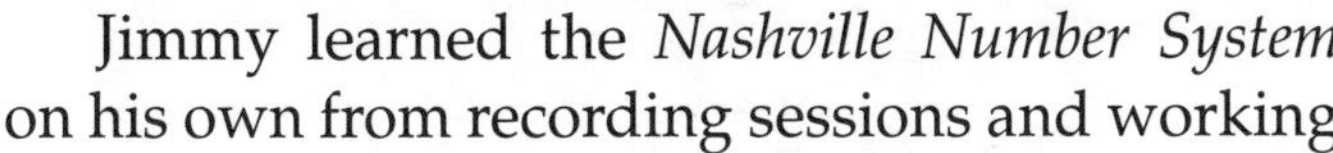

Jimmy learned the *Nashville Number System* on his own from recording sessions and working on television. He humbly says, "My charts may not be musically correct but everybody has their own style of writing them." Jimmy writes a good portion of the charts read by the Grand Ole Opry staff band. His charts correctly contain all the information needed to help the band sound great every night.

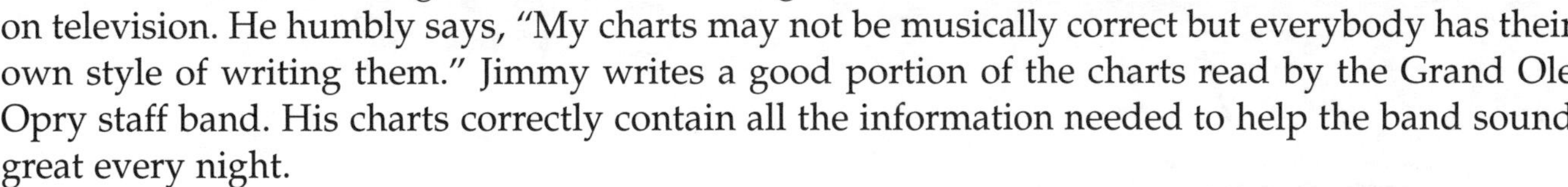

Jimmy writes out the chord changes to the entire song, and to the right of the page, lists the song structure, and which instrument is assigned to handle intro's, fills, turnarounds, and endings. On *Crazy Arms*, he writes the count off to show that there are 2 beats of pickup notes to lead into the intro. Also, Jimmy puts all split bars in parentheses. Odd length measures are also shown in parentheses, and have the appropriate time signatures over them.

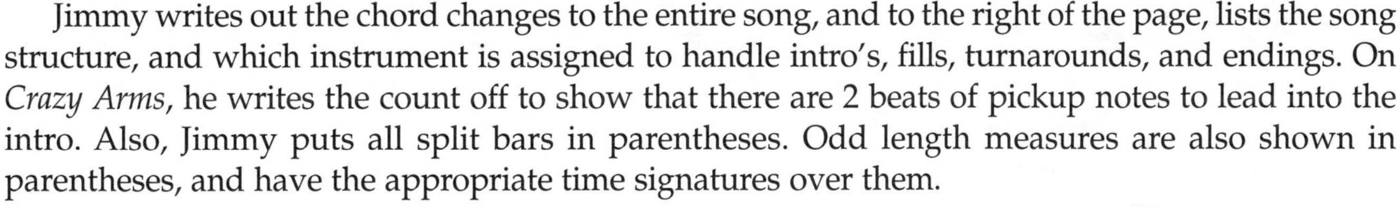

In the first measure of *Crazy*, three hash marks show that the ***1*** chord gets three beats, and a quarter note shows that the ^{b}**7** gets one beat.

For measures where the chord is held, Jimmy uses the bird's eye symbol with slashes over the chord to show how many beats the chord is held.

CRAZY ARMS

count 3412

1 5 1 1

𝄋 1 1 4 1

1 1 5 5

1 1 4 1

1 5 1 1

---

1 1 4 1

1 1 5 5

1 1 4 1 ⊕

1 5 1 1

(TA) 1 5 1 1 D.S. AL CodA

⊕ 1 5 1 1 𝄐

Fills

Intro: Fiddle
V: Steel
C: Fiddle
(TA): Steel
V: Steel
C: Piano

Jimmy Capps

Rocky Top

Banjo Intro
Key (B)

1 (41) (6-5) 1 (1 3/4)

||: 1 (41) (6-5) 1
1 (41) (6-5) 1

1 (41) (6-5) 1
1 (41) (6-5) 1

6-5 7b 4
4 1 (1 7b) 1
(1 7b) 1st 1 (1 3/4 :||

2nd 1

(TA) 1 (41) (6-5) 1
Banjo 1 (41) (6-5) 1

Mand. 6- 5 7b 4
BANJO 4 1 (1 7b) 1 (1 7b) 1 (1 2/4)

1 (41) (6-5) 1
1 (41) (6-5) 1

6- 5 7b 4
4 1 (1 7b) 1
(1 7b) 1
1 1 7b 4 1 1

Jimmy Capps

$\frac{3}{4}$ Key C

LAST CHEATERS WALTZ

$1\ 1^{\Delta}\ 1^{6}\ 5$

1 1 1 1
4 4 4 4
5 5 5 5
5 5 1 1

---

1 1 1 1
4 4 4 4
5 5 5 5
5 5 1 5

$1\ \frac{1}{7}\ \frac{1}{6}\ \frac{1}{5}$
$4\ 4^{6}\ 4^{\Delta}\ 4^{6}$
5 2- 5 5 1 5

$1\ \frac{1}{7}\ \frac{1}{6}\ \frac{1}{5}$
$4\ 4^{6}\ 4^{\Delta}\ 4^{6}$
5 2- 5 5
1 5

(TA) 1 1 1 1
1 1 5 5
$2-\ 2-^{\Delta}\ 2-^{7}\ 5$
5 5 1 5

$1\ \frac{1}{7}\ \frac{1}{6}\ \frac{1}{5}$
$4\ 4^{6}\ 4^{\Delta}\ 4^{6}$
5 2- 5 5 1 5
$1\ \frac{1}{7}\ \frac{1}{6}\ \frac{1}{5}$
$4\ 4^{6}\ 4^{\Delta}\ 4^{6}$
5 2- 5 5 1 5

Fade ||: 1 1 1 1
1 1 5 5
Play out $2-\ 2-^{\Delta}\ 2-^{7}\ 5$
5 5 1 5 :||

Jimmy Capps

6/8 Key (B) MAMAS DON'T LET YOUR BABIES GROW UP TO BE COWBOYS

Intro: 1 1

1 1 4 4
5 5 1 1
1 1 4 4
5 5 5 1 1

1 1 4 4 3/4
5 5 5 (5) 1
1 1 4 4
5 5 5 1 1

Mod To (E)
1 1 4 4
5 5 1 1
1 1 4 4
5 5 5 1 1

𝄆 1 1 4 4 (3/4)
5 5 5 (5) 1
1 1 4 4
5 5 5 1 1 𝄇

V – 1/2 Open
1/2 steel

C – Steel
"MOONEY" Style

Mod

V – 1/2 Open
1/2 steel

C – Steel
Mooney
Style

Jimmy Capps

CRAZY

Piano

1 4 (4 3-) (2- 5)

(1 7b) 6 2- 2-

5 (5 3b°) (1 1#°) (2- 5)

(1 7b) 6 2- 2-

5 5 (1 2-) (3b° 1)

4 (4 4#°) 1 (1 7 1#1)

2 2 5 5

(1 7b) 6 2- 2-

(4 3-) (2- 6/1#) (2- 5) (1 5#) mod

(1 7b) 6 2- 2-

(4 3-) (2- 6/1#) (2- 5) 1 4 1

Jimmy Capps

KEY D Funny How Time Slips Away

Intro Steel

1111

1411
1411
1142
5 (45) (14) 1

(TA) Elect. Guitar
5 (45) (14) (15)

1411
1411
1142
5 (45) (14) 1

(TA) steel
5 (45) (14) (15)

1411
1411
1142
5 (45) (14) 1

Fills

V - 1/2 Steel
1/2 Elect Guitar

(TA) Elect. Guitar

V 1/2 Steel
1/2 Elect Guitar

(TA) steel

V — Piano

Jimmy Capps

Lura Foster

Lura moved to Nashville in 1979 after studying piano and voice for four years at Austin Peay University. Once in Nashville, Lura began working on television shows, *Nashville On the Road* and *Pop Goes The Country*. While with these television shows, Lura met Jerry Whitehurst. It was from Jerry that Lura learned about the *Nashville Number System*. However, she combined her knowledge of formal music notation with the basic number system to derive her own concise and detailed method of translating music to paper.

In 1983, Jerry Whitehurst was hired as musical director of the *Nashville Now* television show. In turn, Jerry hired Lura to write all the charts for the show. "Lura Foster writes the best charts in town", Jerry says. So, since '83, Lura was responsible for all the music that was read and played by the Nashville Now band. Lura says, "It's too bad that some people still scoff at the *Nashville Number System* of writing charts, and think its too simplified." However, her charts contain much more information than many formal charts, since she is arranging for a very large band on one piece of paper.

Lura has developed a few of her own chart writing techniques. For instance, instead of using slashes or parentheses for split bars, she boxes in measures that have more than one chord. The box emphasizes that there is only one measure, and allows room above the chords for rhythmic notation if there is any syncopation. If there is just a straight rhythm, she notates the beats with dots over the chord changes.

Figure 66

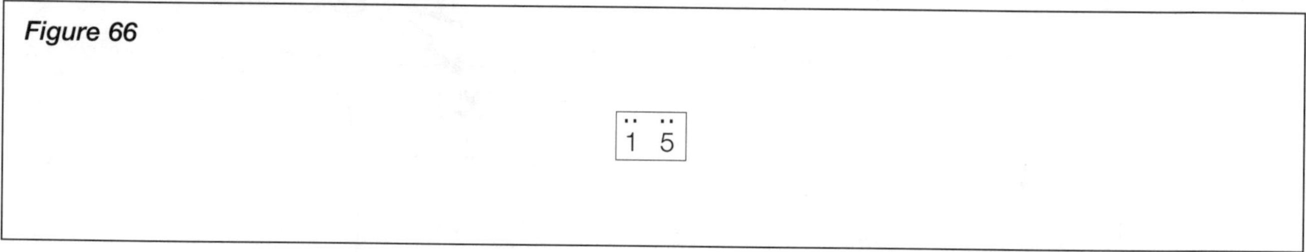

Also, Lura prefers to write out rhythmic figures rather than use diamonds and push signs.

The double slash after a chord 5// means to hit the chord and cut it off.

Another sign Lura uses is an arrow above a melody note pointing up or down to show whether to play the note in a higher or lower octave. Figure 66 is Lura's chart for the intro to *Crazy*.

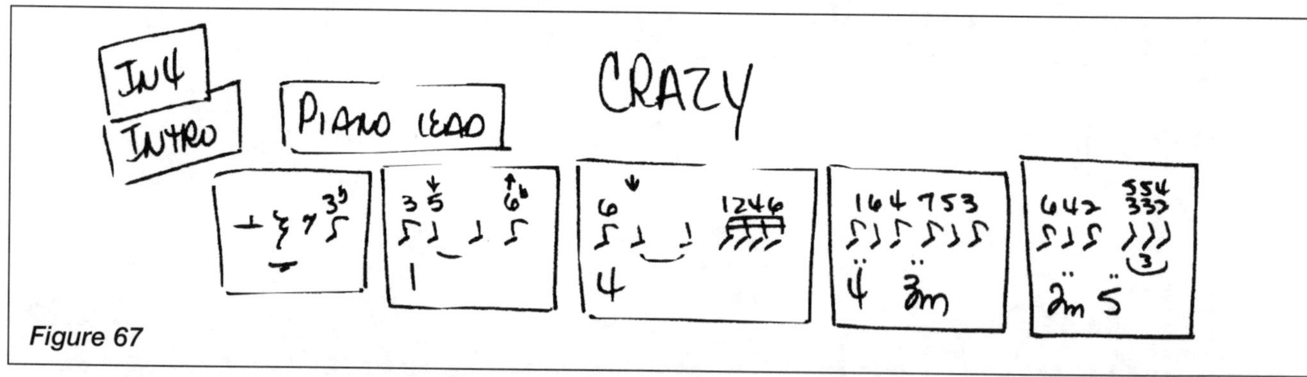

Figure 67

An example of the arrows is in bar 1 of the piano lead. Also, in bar 4 of the intro, notice how she places harmony notes right above the melody notes.

One more example of Lura's use of formal notational symbols is in *Heartbreak Hotel*. She uses a one measure repeat sign ⁒ to indicate that the previous measure is repeated and played exactly as before.

When there are string or horn lines throughout a song, Lura will denote this at the beginning of the chart by writing Str. Cues or Horn Cues.

Lura's charts are meticulous, and look complicated, but she is writing for the rhythm section, strings, and horns all on the same page. Her charts contain a lot of information and must be legible to all the players. Ultimately, the skill of the players, with music communicated with clear charts, make the *Prime Time Country Band*, sound like they played with every featured artist on the original recordings.

In the fall of 1993, Nashville Now left the air to be replaced by *Music City Tonight* (TNN's more up-tempo format for a similar program). The show changed once again to become *Prime Time Country*, and Lura continued to write charts for the house band.

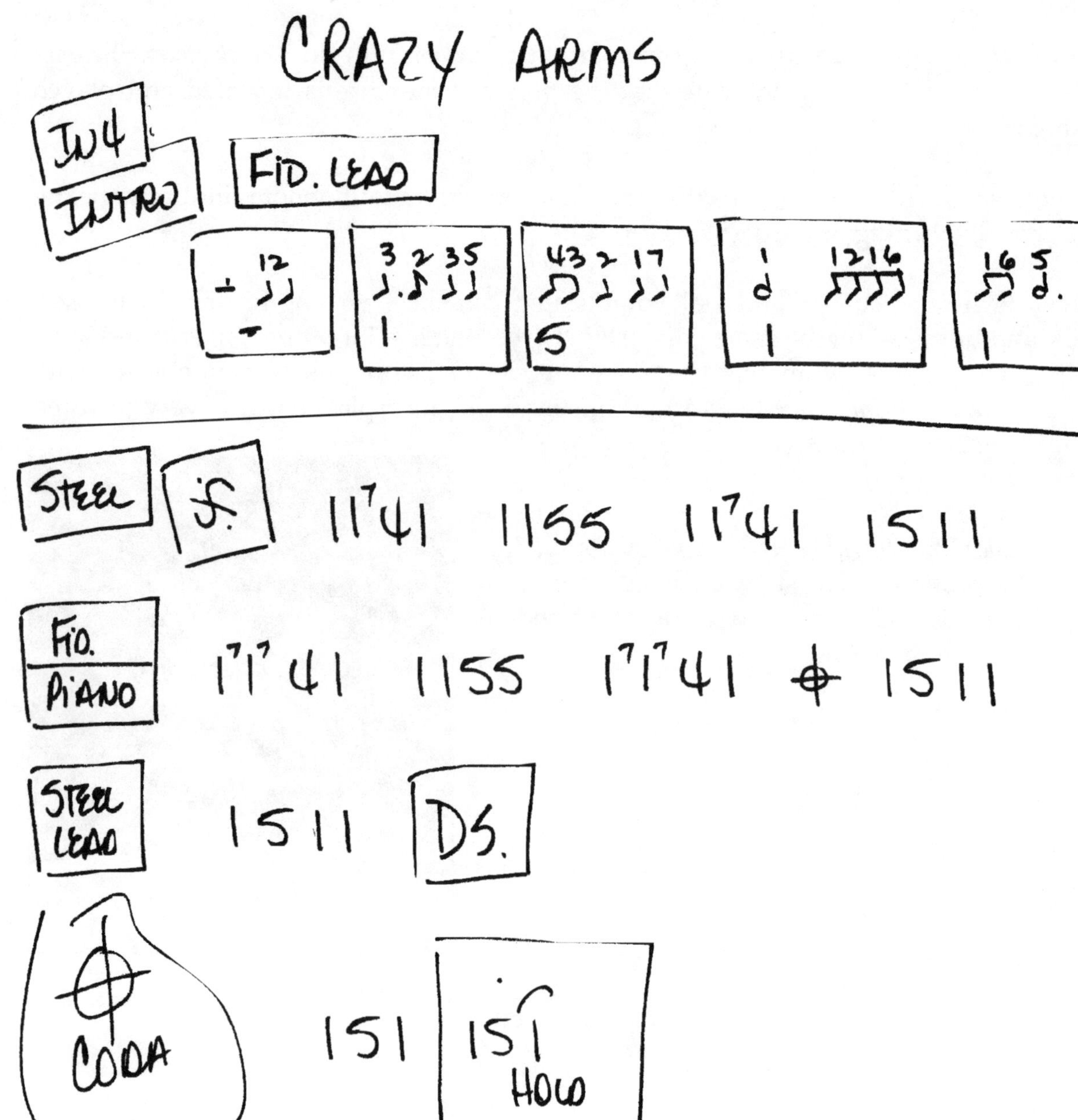

CHART BY:
Laura Foster

HEARTBREAK HOTEL

JN4

VOCAL PICK-UP

BAND

%

BASS ONLY

1- 7b- 6- 5-

4451

BAND

%

BASS ONLY

1- 7b- 6- 5-

BAND

4451

PIANO FILL

1 4451

ELEC LEAD

1111

PIANO LEAD

4451

PIANO FILL

1 445

1 1 7 6 5 4 3 2

HOLD

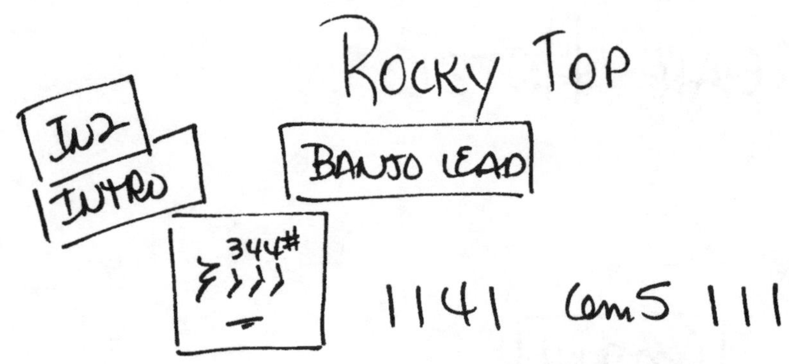

STEEL / BANJO [: 1141 6m511 1141 6m511 :]

STEEL 6m6m55 7b7b44 4411 17b11 17b BANJO 111

STEEL / BANJO [: 1141 6m511 1141 6m511 :]

STEEL 6m6m55 7b7b44 4411 17b11 17b11

BANJO LEAD 1141 6m511 1141 6m511

MAND. LEAD 6m6m55 7b// 7b// 4//& 4//& 4// BANJO LEAD 4411 17b11 17b111

BANJO 1141 6m511 1141 6m511

STEEL 6m6m55 7b7b44 4411 17b11 17b11

11 117b7b 44 11 BANJO 1 1 1/5 1 HOLD 1//

CHART BY:
Laura Foster

LAST CHEATERS WALTZ

IN 3 / INTRO

1 1/7 1/6 | 5 6m 5/7 |

ELEC PIANO / PIANO

[: 1 1/5 1 | 1/5 1 1/5 | 4 4/1 4 4 5 5/2 5 5/2 5 | 5 6m 5/7 | 1 | 5 6m 5/7 | :]

𝄋 1 5/7 6m | 1/5 1/3 | 4 4⁶ 4^Δ | 4⁶/1 4 | 5 2m 5 | 2m 5 | 1 | 5 6m 5/7 |

1 5/7 6m | 1/5 1/3 | 4 4⁶ 4^Δ | 4⁶/1 4 | 5 2m 5 | 2m 5 | 1 | 5 6m 5/7 | ⊕

STG. LEAD

| 5 5-- / 1 | 5 5-- / 1/5 | 56 67 71 / 1 | 3 / 1/5 | 32 1 / 1 | 32 3 / 1 5/7 6m |

| 4 321 / 5 | 71 23 45 / 5 | 6 6-- / 2m | 6 6-- / 1#+ | 671 / 2m/1 | 776 / 5/7 | 5 4#56 / 5 |

| 5 7 / 2m 5 | 135 / 1 | SCALE ↗ / 5 6m 5/7 | D.S.

⊕ CODA

STGS. AS BEFORE

[: 1 1/5 1 1/5 1 | 1 5/7 6m | 5 5 2m 1#+ 2m/1 5/7

5 | 2m 5 | 1 | 5 6m 5/7 | :]

FADE

CHART BY:
Lura Foster

MAMAS, DON'T LET YOUR BABIES GROW UP TO BE COWBOYS

IN FAST 3

INTRO 1 1 1 1

1111 4444 5555 1111

STEEL 1111 4444 5555 55 1111

ELEC [1 1/5 1 1/5 4 4/1 4 4/1 5 5/2 5 5/2 5 5/2

1. 5 1 1/5 :| 2. 1 1/5 1 1 MOD UP 1 STEP

1 1/5 1 1/5 4 4/1 4 4/1 5 5/2 5 5/2 1 1/5 1 1/5

STEEL 1 1/5 1 1/5 4 4/1 4 4/1 5 5/2 5 5/2 5 5/2 1 1/5 1 1/5

ELEC [· 1/5 1 1/5 4 4/1 4 4/1 5 5/2 5 5/2 5 5/2 5 1 1/5

ELEC 1 1/5 1 1/5 4 4/1 4 4/1 5 5/2 5 5/2 5 5/2 1 1/5 1 1/5 ·]

FADE

CHART BY:
Laura Foster

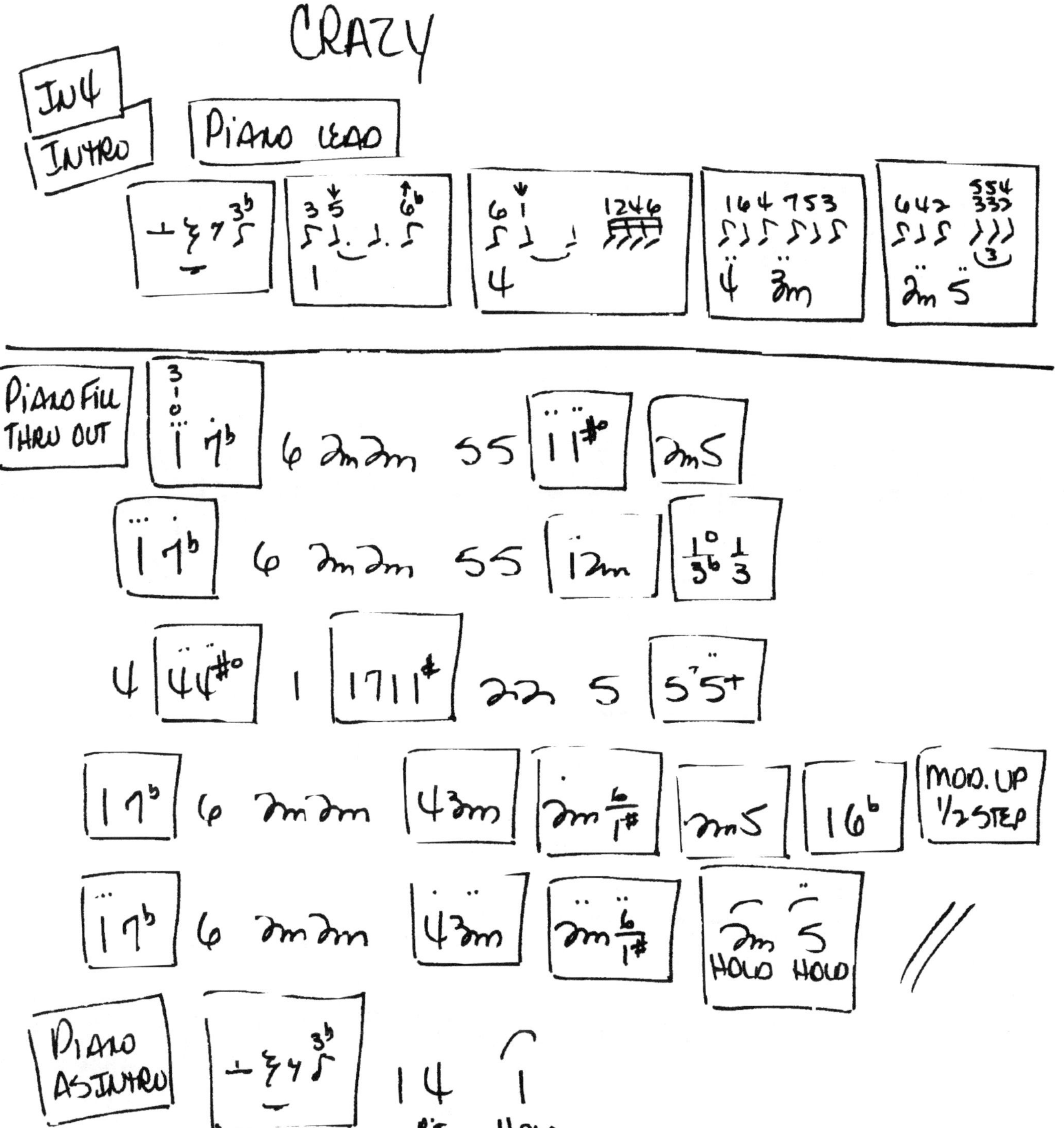

CHART BY: Laura Foster

FUNNY HOW TIME SLIPS AWAY

IN 4

INTRO | STEEL LEAD / ACOUS. FILL |

STEEL & ACOUS. 1 4 1 1 1 4 1 1 (ELEC.) 1 1⁷ 4 2 5 45 14 1

ELEC LEAD 5 45 14 15

STEEL 1 4 1 1 1 4 1 1 (ELEC) 1 1⁷ 4 2 5 45 14 1

ELEC LEAD 5 45 14 15

PIANO 1 4 1 1 1 4 1 1 1 1⁷ 4 2 5 45 (STEEL) 14 | 15+ 1⁶ HOLD |

CHART BY:

Laura Foster

Barry Beckett

Barry Beckett is from Birmingham, Alabama. He studied 3 semesters of music theory at the University of Alabama, then left school to play piano in bands around the southeast. A D.J. named Don Shroeder, took Barry and a couple of his band members to record some demos in Muscle Shoals and they cut their first record: *I'm Your Puppet*, by James and Bobby Purify.

In 1967, Barry was invited to move to Muscle Shoals and become the staff pianist in the soon to be famous Muscle Shoals Rhythm Section. His first record to play on after he began working in Muscle Shoals was by Mike Bloomfield. Thousands of recording sessions that Barry participated on included a tremendous variety of material, including work with Wilson Pickett, Clarence Carter, King Curtis, and John Hammond. Number charts were used on all these sessions.

Due to his highly organized and easy to follow style, Barry ended up writing chord charts for many of the sessions, and introduced the type of chart that has become standard in the Muscle Shoals recording community. Notice how Barry underlines split bars and puts hash marks over the chord to show how many beats the chord gets. He underlines split bars so there is no mark on the page that interferes with the flow of the chart. Also Barry puts parentheses around chords that are held as diamonds. Notice how he labels each section of the song alphabetically so there is no question as to the order of each section, even though there may be repeats and codas. For *Heartbreak Hotel*, Barry devised his own sign, the X, over the chord where the musicians should continue counting, but not play.

Beckett says that a couple of real ground breaking records to come out of Muscle Shoals were with Paul Simon and Bob Seger. All the musical parts that the Muscle Shoals band came up with were ad libbed around number charts. In 1973, Quincy Jones hired Barry for a session because of the great feel he has in his playing. Barry explained to Quincy that he could not read music very well. Quincy said that was no problem, but handed Barry a multi-paged and complex arrangement written in traditional notation. To help deal with a tricky modulation in an unfamiliar key, Barry translated the arrangement to numbers. He successfully mastered the Quincy Jones session in L.A. with a *Nashville Number System* chart. Beckett has proven that the number system is valid all around the country with any style of music.

In 1984, because of differing music direction in Muscle Shoals, Barry moved to Nashville. He said that because of his rock and roll and R&B background he wasn't offered any production work for a while. Finally, Jim Ed Norman, Bill Carter, and Jack Bermley called Barry to produce Shelly West and show what he could do with a country act. The results were country records with a harder hitting sound and punch that was very successful. Since, Barry has produced many of Hank Williams Jr.'s records as well as Alabama's album, *Southern Star*. Barry also enjoyed producing for Lorrie Morgan because of the satisfaction of breaking a new act. Barry likes the *Nashville Number System*.

CRAZY ARMS

INTRO

1	5	1	1 5 6 7

= (A) (B)

$.	1	1	4	1
	1	1	5	5
	1	1	4	1
	1	5	1	1

= CHORUS

1	1	4	1	
1	1	5	5	
1	7	4	1	⊕
1	5	1	1 5 6 7	

= INST

1	5	1	1 5 6 7	D.S.

⊕ = ENDING

1	5	1	1 5 (1) (1)

Heartbreak Hotel

[illegible]

(A) (1) 1 1 (1) 1 1 (1) 1

4 4 5 1

(B)(C)(D) 3X [illegible] (1) 1 1 (1) 1 1 (1) 1

4 4 5 1

= [illegible]

1 1 1 1

4 4 5 1

(E) (1) 1 1 (1) (1) [illegible] 1

4 4 5 (1) = (1) 2 (1)

Rocky Top

INTRO

1 41 6-5 1 1 (2/4)

A C

𝄆 1 41 6-5 1

1 41 6-5 1

$ = B D E

1 41 6-5 1

1 41 6-5 1

= CHORUS

6- 5 7^b 4

4 1 ⊕

17^b 1 17^b 1 1 (2/4) 𝄇

= INST.

1 41 6-5 1

1 41 6-5 1

6- 5 (7^b)(6^b) 44(4)

4 1

17^b 1 17^b 1 1 (2/4) D.S.

⊕ = 17^b 1 17^b 1 1

= ENDING

1 7^b 4 1 1 (1) (1) (1)

Cheater's

INTRO 1 7/3- 6/1 5 6- 7/2

= (A)

1 1 4 4

5 5 5 1 5 6- 7/5

1 1 1^7 4 4

5 5 5 1 5 6 7/5

CHORUS

1 7/3- 6 5^7 4 4^6 4 4^6

5 2 5 1 5 6- 7/2

1 7/3- 6 5^7 4 4^6 4 4^6

5 2- 5 1 5 6 7/5

INST

1 1 1 5

2- 2^{b+5} 4/1 5/7 5 1 5 6 7/5

= CHORUS

1 7/3- 6 5^7 4 4^6 4 4^6

5 2- 5 1 5 6- 7/5

1 7/3- 6/1 5 4 4^6 4 4^6

5 2 5 1 5 6 7/5

= INST FADE

R- 1 1 1 5

2 2^{b+5} 4/1 5/7 5 1 5 6- 7/2

COWBOYS

6/8 INTRO

1 1

‖: = (A) (B)

MOD 1 STEP 1 1 4 4

5 5 1 1

1 1 4 4

5 5 5 1 1

= CHORUS

1 1 4 4

5 5 5 5 (3/8) 1

1 1 4 4

5 5 5 1 1 :‖ MOD 1 STEP AT (B)

= CHORUS + FADE

‖: 1 1 4 4

5 5 5 5 (3/8) 1

1 1 4 4

5 5 5 1 1 :‖

CRAZY

INTRO

1 4 43- 2-5^{c}

= (A)

"1 17^{b} 6 2- 2-

5 53^{bo} 11$^{\#o}$ 2-5^{c}

"1 17^{b} 6 2- 2-

5 5 12-^{7} 3^{bo}/3

= BRIDGE

4 44$^{\#o}$ 1 1711$^{\#}$

2 2 5 55^{+5}

= (B)

"1 17^{b} 6 2- 2-

43- 2-2^{bo} 2-5^{c} 16

MOD 1 = (C)

117^{b} 6 2- 2-

43- 2-2^{bo} RIT. (2-)(5^{c})

= ENDING

1 "4^{7} 4^{7} 4^{7} RIT. (1)

HE STOPPED LOVING HER

=(A)

1	1 2- 1/3	4	4
5	5	1	1
1	1 2- 1/3	4	4
5	5	1	(5⁷)

L=(B)

MOD 2

1	1 2- 1/3	4	4
5	5	1	1
1	1 2- 1/3	4	4
5	5	1	1 5 6- 5/7

=CHORUS

1	1 2- 1/3	4	4
5	5	(1)	(1)

=

1	1 2- 1/3	4	4
5	5	1	1 5 6- 5/7

CHORUS

1	1 2- 1/3	4	4
5	RET (5)		

RET.

1	(1)

Buchart

Eddie Bayers

Eddie Bayers is from Peutaxant, Maryland. He studied classical piano beginning at age 7 and continued to study classical and jazz music at Laney College and later at the University of California at Berkeley. To get through school, Eddie played soul and R&B music at night in bands like the Checkmates LTD. He later worked with gospel singer Edwin Hawkins.

In 1973, Eddie moved to Nashville and worked for about two years as a keyboard player. At age 24, he was playing keys on a gig in Nashville's Printer's Alley with Larrie Londin. Eddie says Larrie inspired him to switch over to drums as his main instrument.

This was early in a huge career in which Eddie has recorded with an endless list of major artists including Alan Jackson, Bob Seger, John Fogerty, Suzy Boguss, Tricia Yearwood, The Judds, and Wynonna. A few career stats earned by Eddie Bayers: He has played on 96 Gold or Platinum albums; Won *Academy of Country Music* Drummer of the year for '92 and '93; *Music Row's* #1 drummer; The most Top Ten Albums in *Billboard* Magazine every year since 1989; *Modern Drummer* Magazine's #1 Country Drummer for '93; 3 CMA Awards for playing on the single of the year, and one Musician of the Year Nomination.

When Eddie moved to Nashville he had never worked with the *Nashville Number System*. However, from classical studies he knew about the use of Roman numerals and figured bass. The first Nashville charts Eddie experienced didn't utilize formal music notation. Then he saw Dennis Burnside write rhythm charts using numbers combined with formal notation. Other stylistic differences he noticed were the different kinds of split bar notations and codes for pushes and 2/4 bars. Look at Eddie's charts and notice his split bars with 2 beats per chord are divided with a diagonal slash. However, his other split bars are in parentheses and many have notation to show rhythmic changes. Also, like Beckett, Eddie uses x's over rhythm notes to show stops. Eddie says "It was interesting to watch how everybody dealt with their own ways of using the Nashville system. As I got into more sessions, the leaders of the sessions or the producer passed out your chart and you'd see little things. Then it's a matter of inquiring, "What's this?"

"The number system is so valid. There really isn't any other form to me as far as basic recording or even learning a song. Once you learn the system, it makes total sense. Especially in a transposition situation." Eddie tells, "It's funny how people get biased. I remember working with Mike Post who had everything notated out when you worked for him. When working out certain modulations he always made the joke, "Let's see them write this out in numbers." "The thing was," Eddie says, "it can be written out in numbers, easy. Basically by using the English language, like: 'Mod to the ♭3, or the ***1*** equals the ***4***, or whatever. I've never seen the number system not being able to be used." Eddie used number charts on the '93 Bob Seger album, *Fire Inside*, and John Fogerty's '93 album; a couple more examples of non Nashville type sessions.

For drummers new to Nashville, Eddie suggests, "Try to learn charts that others are using. Find your own method until you are able to start realizing how to utilize what everybody else is doing." Eddie used to watch Larrie Londin years ago write a chart full of ***1***'s to represent chord changes, then notate kicks accordingly. "If the job gets done, to me that's the bottom line; however you can get to the situation of learning a song as quick as possible and being able to play it."

CRAZY ARMS

INTRO 1 5 1 (1 5 6 - 5/7)

VS - 1 1 4 1
1 1 5 5
1 1 4 1
1 5 1 1

CH) 1 1 4 1
1 1 5 5
1 1 4 1 ⊕
1 5 1 (1 5 6 - 5/7) DC al coda

⊕ 1 5 1 (1 5 1)

Eddie
Bayers

Heartbreak Hotel

Vocal Pickup

4 4 5 1

3x

4 4 5 1

INST —

4 4 5 1

4 4 5

Eddie Bayers

Rocky Top ( ) = 2/4

INTRO 1 4/1 6/5 1 (1)

𝄋 1 4/1 6/5 1

1 4/ 6/5 1

$ 1 4/1 6-/5 1

1 4/ 6/5 1

(CH) 6 - 5 b7 4

4 1 ⊕

1/b7 1 1/b7 1 1x (1) 𝄋

INST 1 4/ 6/5 1

1 4/1 6/5 1

6 5 b7 4

4 1

1/b7 1 1/b7 1 (1) Dr al coda

⊕ 1/b7 1 1/b7 1 1

1 b7 4 1 (1 ?) Goodie Bayer

Last Cheaters Waltz

INTRO 1/3/7 (1/6 5 6- 5/7)

VS) 1 1 4 4
5 5 5 (1 5 6 5/7)
1 1/3 4 4
5 5 5 (1 5 6 5/7)

CH) 1/3/7 6/5 4 4
5/2 5 (1 5 6 5/7)
1/3/7 6/5 4 4
5/2 5 (1 5 6 5/7)

INST 1 1 1 5
2/2 6 4/5/7 5 (1 5 6- 5/7)

CH) 1/3/7 6/5 4 4
5/2 5 (1 5 6 5/7)
1/3/7 6/5 4 4
5/2 5 (1 5 6 5/7)

Short B. 1 1 1 5
2/2 6 4/5/7 5 (1 5 6 5/7)

Eddie Bayers

Mamas

( ) = 3/8

6/8 1 1

𝄋 1 1 4 4

5 5 1 1

1 1 4 4

5 5 5 1 1

CH) 1 1 4 4

5 5 5 (5) 1

1 1 4 4

5 5 5 1 1 𝄋 mod 1 step on repeat

CHORUS 𝄋 1 1 4 4

5 5 5 (5) 1

1 1 4 4

5 5 5 1 1 𝄋

Edward Bayer

CRAZY

INTRO 1 4 4/3- 2-/5

(1 1 7) 6 2- 2-

5 5/3^{60} 1/1$^{\#}$ 2-/5

(1 1 7) 6 2- 2-

5 5 1/2- ^{b}3/3

CH) 4 4/4$^{\#o}$ 1 1

2 2 5 5/5^{+5}

(1 1 7) 6 2- 2-

4/3- 2-/2^{60} 2-/5 1/6 mod ½ step

(1 1 7) 6 2- 2-

4/3- 2-/2^{60} 2- 5

RIT

OUTRO 1 4 1

Eddie Bayers

Funny

INTRO 1 1 1 1

1 4 1 1

1 4 1 1

1 1 4 2

5 4/5 1/4 1

T/A 5 4/5 1/4 1/5

1 4 1 1

1 4 1 1

1 1 4 2

5 4/5 1/4 1

2 T/A 5 4/5 1/4 1/5

1 4 1 1

1 4 1 1

1 1 4 2 1 1 4

5 4/5 1/4 1

Eddie Bayers

Brent Mason

In 1981 Brent's wife Kirstin cashed in her life insurance policy to finance their move to Nashville from his hometown of Grover Hill, Ohio. Brent met with friend Paul Franklin, his only industry contact, and through Paul's brother-in-law, got a gig at the Stage Coach Lounge. Brent quickly earned a reputation for being a great guitarist while working at the Stagecoach. One night, Brent noticed Chet Atkins had brought George Benson in to hear him play. Soon after, Brent's first master session in Nashville was for Chet's *Stay Tuned* album.

Today, Brent is one of the most demanded session guitarists in Nashville. He's played on over 100 gold and platinum albums in the past ten years; albums by Alan Jackson, Trisha Yearwood, Brooks and Dunn, The Mavericks, and George Strait. The Academy of Country Music named him "Guitarist of the Year" for 1993 - 1995 and the CMA has nominated Brent for "Musician of the Year" 1993 - 1996.

Brent says, "I learned the number system from picking in the Nashville clubs. When you didn't know the songs, fellow players would hold up their hand and finger the numbers - 1,2,3,4,5 etc. before each change (during the song). If there was a ♭7, I guess you were out of luck!" "I learned more about the *Nashville Number System* as I got into recording sessions."

Brent Mason charts are very clean. Notice he writes across the page in 4 bar phrases. He uses the D.S. al 𝄌 sign and repeat signs and they are clearly marked for finding your way around the song. Brent underlines split bars and notates rhythmic passages instead of using any shorthand abbreviations. Finally, take a look at *Crazy*. Brent charted the more typical night club arrangement of the song. Notice he uses a half note instead of a diamond over the 5+ on the bridge. This is probably the version of *Crazy* you'll be playing at any of the nightclubs in Nashville.

Check out Brent's guitar instructional video from Hotlicks Productions. It was released May 1996 and quickly became one of their best selling videos. Also, in the spring of 1997, Mercury Records released an album of Brent's original instrumentals, called"Hot Wired".

"Crazy Arms"

Intro: 1 5 1 1 (1 5 6 7)

Vrs. ||: 1 1⁷ 4 1 1 1 5 5

1 1⁷ 4 1 1 5 1 1

Chrs. 1 1⁷ 4 1 1 1 5 5

1 1⁷ 4 1 1 5 1 1 | 1. 1 5 1 1 (1 5 6 7) :||

Tag 1 5 1 1 5 1

Bert Mann

"HeartBreak Hotel"

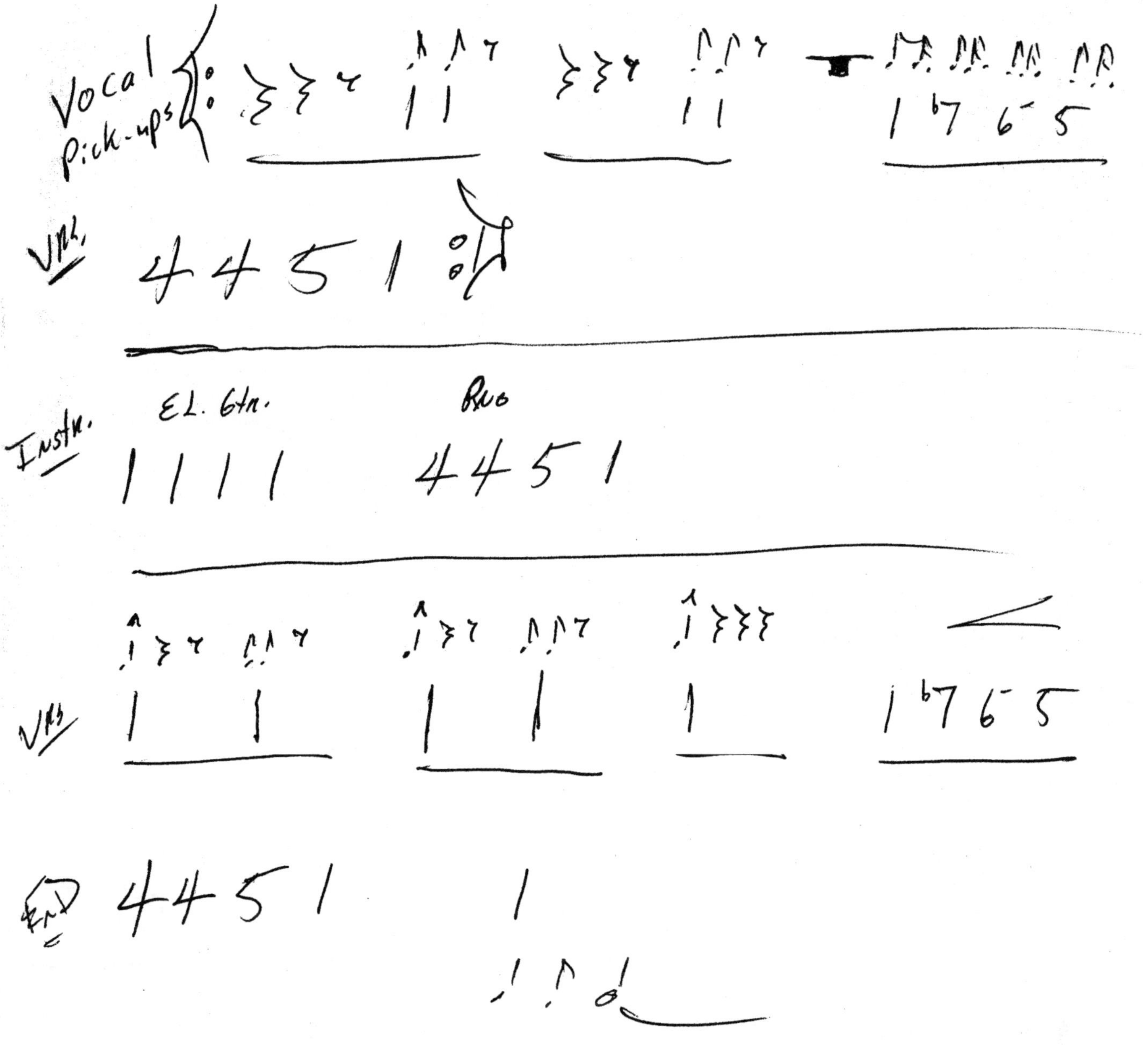

Vocal Pick-ups

1 1 — 1 1 — 1 b7 6 5

Vrs.

4 4 5 1

Instr.

El. Gtr. — 1 1 1 1

Pno — 4 4 5 1

Vrs — 1 1 — 1 1 — 1 — 1 b7 6 5

End 4 4 5 1 — 1

Bert S. Moon

"Rocky Top"

Intro: 1 1 4 1 6- 5 1 1

(V.) 𝄆 1 1 4 1 6- 5 1 1 1 1 4 1 6- 5 1 1

𝄋 1 1 4 1 6- 5 1 1 1 1 4 1 6- 5 1 1

(C.) 6- 6- 5 5 b7 b7 4 4 4 4 1 1 1 b7 1 1

1 b7 1 1 ⊕ 𝄇

Instr. 1 1 4 1 6- 5 1 1 1 1 4 1 6- 5 1 1

6- 6- 5 5 b7 b7 4 4 4 4 1 1 1 b7 1 1 1 b7 1 1

D.S. al coda

⊕ Tag 1 1 . 1 1 b7 b7 4 4 1 1 1 1

Bart Mason

"Last Cheater's Waltz"

3/4

Intro 1 1△ 1⁶ 5↗

VRS. 1 1111 4444 5555 55 1 1 (567↗)

VRS. 2 1111 4444 5555 55 1 1 (567↗)

CHRS. 𝄋 1 5/7 6⁻ 1/5 4 4⁶ 4△ 4⁶ 5 2⁻ 5 5 1 1 (567↗)

1 5/7 6⁻ 1/5 4 4⁶ 4△ 4⁶ 5 2⁻ 5 5 ⊕ 1 5↗

Solo 1111 1155 2⁻ 2⁻△ 2⁻⁷ 5/7 55 1 5↗

D.S.

⊕ 1 5 6⁻ 5/7 1̂

Rit

"CowBoys"

Intro: 1 1 1 1

V. ‖: 1 1 1 1 4444 5555 1111

1111 4444 5555 5511 . 11

C. 1111 4444 5555 5551 . 1

1111 4444 5555 5511 . 11 :‖ MOD ↗ ①

V

C MOD

V

C Fade

Bret Mann

"Crazy"

Intro: 1 4 4 3⁻ 2⁻ 5

Vrs. 1 6 2⁻ 2⁻ 5 5 5⁺ 1 1#° 2⁻ 5

1 6 2⁻ 2⁻ 5⁷ 5⁷ 1 2⁻ 3♭° 1/3

Br. 𝄋 4 4 4#° 1 1 7 1 1# 2 2 5 2⁻ 5 5⁺ ⊕

Vrs. 1 6 2⁻ 2⁻ 4 3⁻ 2⁻ 6/1# 2⁻ 5 1 5

Solo's 1 6 2⁻ 2⁻ 5 5 1 1#° 2⁻ 5

1 6 2⁻ 2⁻ 5 5 1 2⁻ 3♭° 1/3 DS al coda

⊕ 1 6 2⁻ 2⁻ 4 3⁻ 2⁻ 6/1# 2⁻ 5 1 1⁷

4 3⁻ 2⁻ 6/1# 2⁻ 5 you.... 1

Bart Mann

"Night club version" ☺

"Funny How Time Slips"

Intro 1 1 1 1

(V.) 1 4 1 1 1 4 1 1

1 1^7 4 2 5 45 14 1

T.A. 5 5 1 5↗

(V.) 1 4 1 1 1 4 1 1

1 1^7 4 2 5 45 1 1 ↘

T.A. 5 5 1 5↗

(V.) 1 4 1 1 1 4 1 1 1 1^7 4 2 5 45 14 1 #1 1

1511

The cd, 1511 (*"Fifteen Eleven"*), contains 9 songs with several different styles represented. These songs give an opportunity to write charts which demonstrate many of the number system tools. The idea is to watch the bars go by as you listen to the music. For example, you will hear how to count a *"diamond"* while you see how it's drawn on the chart; or listen to a syncopated rhythm as you count the beats. With the cd, you will see and *feel* how to count bars.

In this section of the book, I'm going to talk about the chart for each song from the cd and some of the chart's intricacies. This way, you'll be able to understand why I used certain styles of charting. I'll also try to explain how you would discuss this music with a fellow musician in the Nashville language. So, if someone yells, " *Fifteen Eleven* " across the stage, you'll know they're probably talking about the chords to a song intro or turnaround.

A few of these charts are pretty advanced, but they will make a lot of sense as you listen to the tunes. For instance, on songs like Civil War and The Seam, I've written charts that show pretty detailed arrangements. Claire's Pet Shop, on the other hand, has a simple arrangement and fairly basic chord chart.

Some of these songs are not what one would usually expect to see as a Nashville number chart. The 6/4 rock tune, Northern Pike, is a little more rhythmically and harmonically busy than the George Jones song, He Stopped Loving Her Today. So, we have a chance to see *the number system* at work in a more complex situation. I've also included some very simple songs and charts, like The Shuffle Board. So, I'm sure you will find alot you can use for charting your own songs.

Slide Guitar

Slide Guitar is a straight 8th's rock style tune; nothing fancy. The first thing I would point out, however, is that the lead instrument (slide guitar) anticipates or pushes alot of down beats. Listen to the rhythm section, though. They mostly play straight, underneath the pushes. These are sometimes called right handed pushes, referring to a piano player's right hand as the lead instruments and the left hand as the rhythm section. I didn't notate the right handed pushes; only pushes that the band plays together.

I used repeats for verse 2 and chorus 2 because it saves space on the chart and the rhythm section plays each section identically anyway.

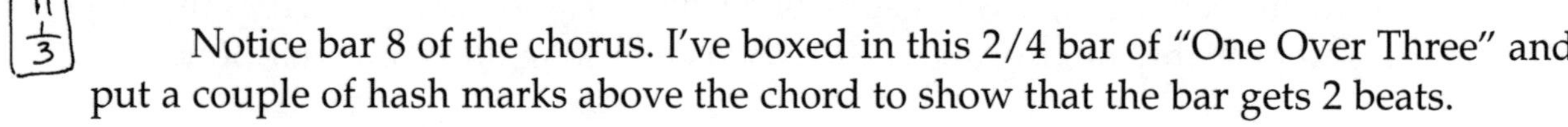

Notice bar 8 of the chorus. I've boxed in this 2/4 bar of "One Over Three" and put a couple of hash marks above the chord to show that the bar gets 2 beats.

After the last bar of the 2nd Chorus, we modulate "Up to **4** ". In other words, the **4** chord becomes the new key or new ***1*** . The Chorus is in the key of D. Therefore, the next section will be in the key of ***G*** and the first chord of the Bridge will be a ***C*** chord. Likewise, at the end of the Bridge, we modulate "Down to **5** ". The ***5*** of the Bridge key ***(G)*** becomes the new ***1*** for the following section (Verse 3). So, Verse 3 is in the key of ***D*** and it's first chord is a ***B-*** .

Finally, look at bars 9 and 10 of the last Chorus (*Figure 67*). Here, the band actually anticipates with the slide guitar, so I've marked these bars with a push.

Figure 67

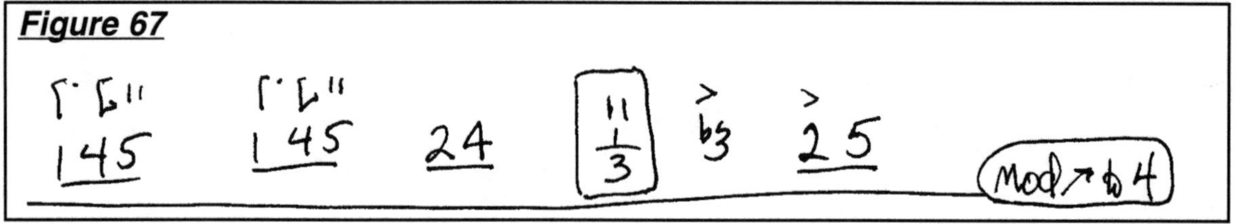

Slide Guitar

Chas Williams

(D) 4/4

8ths Rock

♩=122

[V] ||: 6-3 | 24 | 145 | 24
6-3 | 24 | 145 | 24

[C] 145 | 145 | 145 | 24
145 | 145 | 24 | 1/3 | b3 | 25 :|| (Mod ↗ to 4)

Key (G)

[B] 415 | 1 | 415 | 1
415 | 3 | 415 | 1 (Mod ↘ to 5)

Key (D)
Breakdown
Slide Acapella

[V] 6-3 | 24 | 145 | 24
6-3 | 24 | 145 | 24

[C] 145 | 145 | 145 | 24
145 | 145 | 145 | 24

[C] 145 | 145 | 145 | 24
145 | 145 | 24 | 1/3 | >b3 | >25 (Mod ↗ to 4)

Key (G)

[B] ||: 415 | 1 | 415 | 1
415 | 3 | 415 | 1 :|| Vamp 'til Fade

The Seam

For the chart, The Seam, I'm going to tell you the whole first verse (Figure 68) as if we were in a session and you were taking dictation:

"There are 4 beats of pick ups by the guitar. The first line is: One. One. A two-four bar of Six Minor split Five. Four. Four split Two Minor, split One, with two beats on the Four chord. Line two is: Five over Seven. Five split One over Three, with three beats on the Five chord. Four. Five diamond. The last bar is a two-four bar of rest."

(Notice for the last bar I just wrote the "top hat" symbol for a 2 beat rest and put it in a box. I didn't use any hash marks since the rest symbol tells how many beats.)

Figure 68

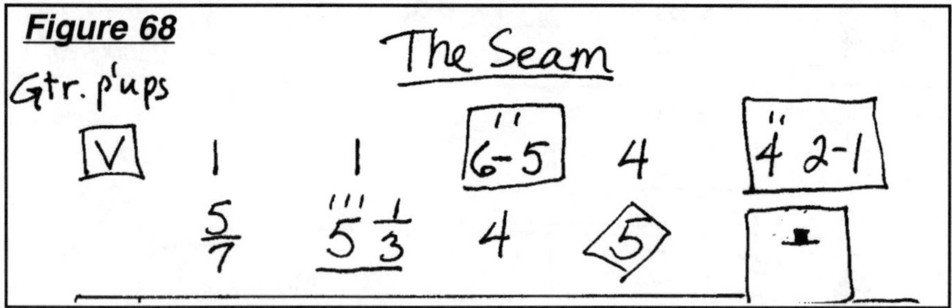

After verse 3, we modulate up to the **4** chord for the Channel. **4** in the key of C becomes ***1*** in the key of F. However, the first chord of the Channel is a ***4***^{7} or Bb^{7}. Bar 8 of the Channel is used to modulate up to the **2** of F. The *"sharp Four seventh"*, or B^{7}, moves us nicely to the E- or ***6-*** in the key of G for the Bridge.

There is a deliberate ritard through the last bar of the Bridge before we modulate up to **4** (the original song key) and the Solos section. Here, the feel changes from 8ths ballad to a cut time -hip hop feel. Notice that even though the pulse and tempo of the song doubles, the chart continues to be counted with quarter notes at the original tempo of 90 bpm.

Bar 4 of the Solos section is 2 beats of *"Two over Sharp Four"*, then a unison rhythm section lick.

Look at *Figure 69* , the last line of the Solos section. Notice the eigth note tied to the fourth bar. This is just another way to write a push for that **4**. The last bar of the line is a *"5$^{7\,13}$ with a Birdseye"*. So, we hold that chord until the guitar cues with the pickups to Verse 4.

Figure 69

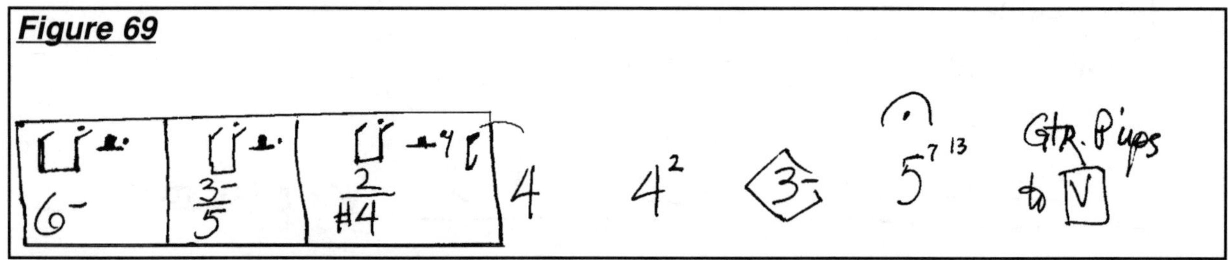

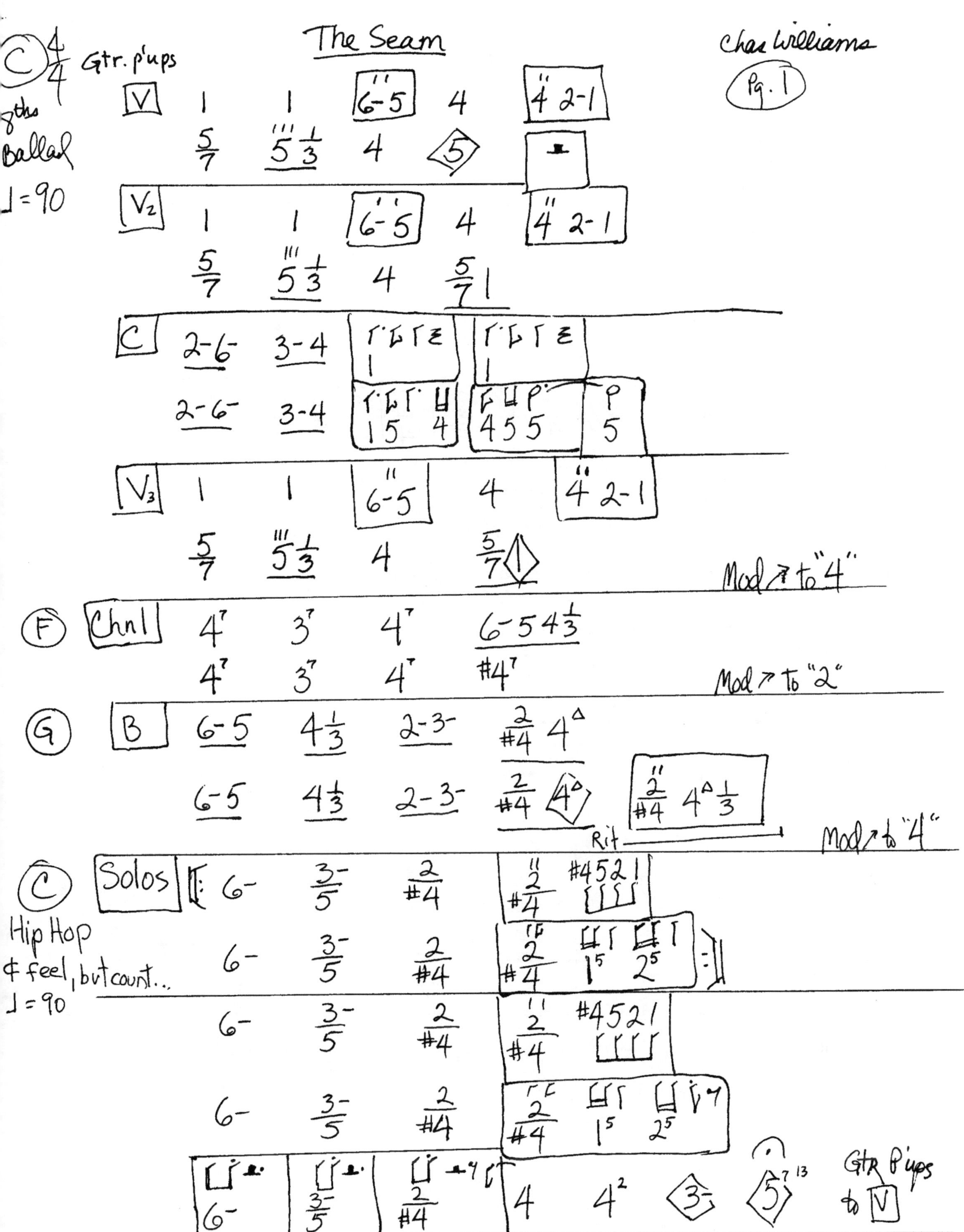
The Seam
Chas Williams
Pg. 1
C 4/4 Gtr. p'ups
8ths Ballad
♩=90
V
V2
C
V3
Mod ↗ to "4"
F Chnl
Mod ↗ to "2"
G B
Rit
Mod ↗ to "4"
C Solos
Hip Hop
¢ feel, but count...
♩=90
Gtr P'ups to V

The Seam

Chas Williams

Pg. 2

C 4/4

8ths

V4 1 1 [6-5] 4 4 2-1

5/7 5 1/3 4 5/7 1

C 2-6 3-4 [rhythm] [rhythm]

2-6 3-4 1 5 4 | 4 5 5 | 5

V5 1 1 [6-5] 4 4 2-1

5/7 5 1/3 4 5/7 1

Tag 4 [5] 1

Rit.

Claire's Pet Shop

by Char Williams

Ⓒ ¢
♩= 144
Halftime feel w/ swing

V	𝄆 6-4	51	6-4	1		Dobro Lead
	6-4	51	6-4	1		
C	1	1	1	6-4		2nd X GTR. Lead
	1	6-	3-4	51		
	1	1	1	6-4		
	1	6-	3-4	51 𝄇		
B	3	6-4	5	TBA 2- 1		
	3	6-4	5	1		
	2-1	5	15	4		
	2-1	5	15	4	4 45	Unison
Breaks down Bass + Drums Out — V	6-4	51	6-4	1		
	6-4	51	6-4	1		
All In * — C	1	1	1	6-4		Dobro + GTR. Trade
	1	6-	3-4	51		
	1	1	1	6-4		
	1	6-	3-4	51		
TAG	3-4	51 𝄐				

Claire's Pet Shop

Claire's Pet Shop is a good example of a song with a halftime feel that is counted in cut time. Quarter notes equal 144 bpm, so you're counting a fast 4 beat bar, but playing with a halftime swinging feel. Otherwise, the chart should be easy to follow while listening to the cd.

Sal Mineo

Sal Mineo has a latin feel and is written in 2/4 . There are a few events that may be challenging to keep up with in this song. First, every section is in a different key; a lot of modulating. At the end of verses 1,2 and 3, the song modulates to the verse's **5** chord for the Chorus. The Choruses however start with their own **5** chord. So, for the Choruses, we're not only modulating to the Verse's **5** , but the **5** of **5** . So, the Choruses start on a B chord since we're in the key of E .

Notice at the repeat, how the 1st X we go back to the Verse, so we mod up to **4**, the original key. For the 2nd X, however, we go to the Bridge and mod down to ***b7*** .

Chorus 3 is a little different because it is slightly reharmonized, though the melody is the same.

Following the last Chorus is a half Verse. Bar 8 of this Verse is wierd because there is a modulation right in the middle of the bar.(*Figure 70*) So, I made it into two half measures. You play the quarter note on the ***1*** chord, which is a 1/4 bar. Then you mod up to ***4*** to play the band unison lick, which is also a 1/4 bar.

Figure 70

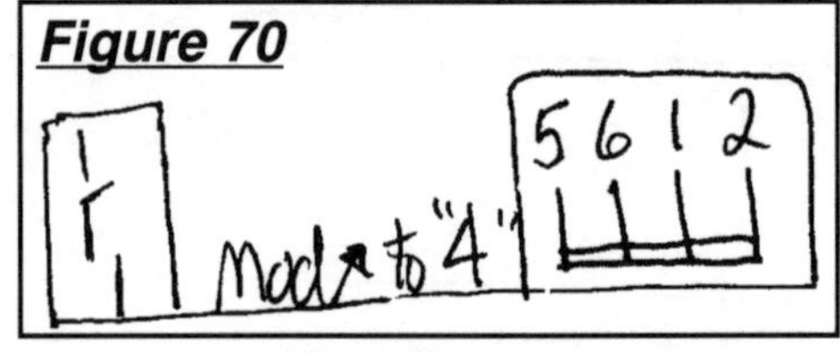

The lick is actually working in the key of D and it takes you to the Bridge, which is in the key of D. The lick would look strange written from the Verse key of A , so I chose to write it in the key in which it functions.

Finally, we come to the 2nd Bridge and Outro. I must say, this is the first time I've ever changed formats in the middle of a chart. The reason I started writing across the page is, not only am I running out of paper, but also, the Bridge is in 8 bar phrases. So instead of having 2 columns of 4 bars, the player can look at each 8 bar phrase as a single unit with it's own instructions. Also, with all the repeating ***1*** 's in this section, writing across the page seems to be an easy way to count bars in groups of 8. I still like to write columns of 4 bars, but this situation seemed to call for some creative space management.

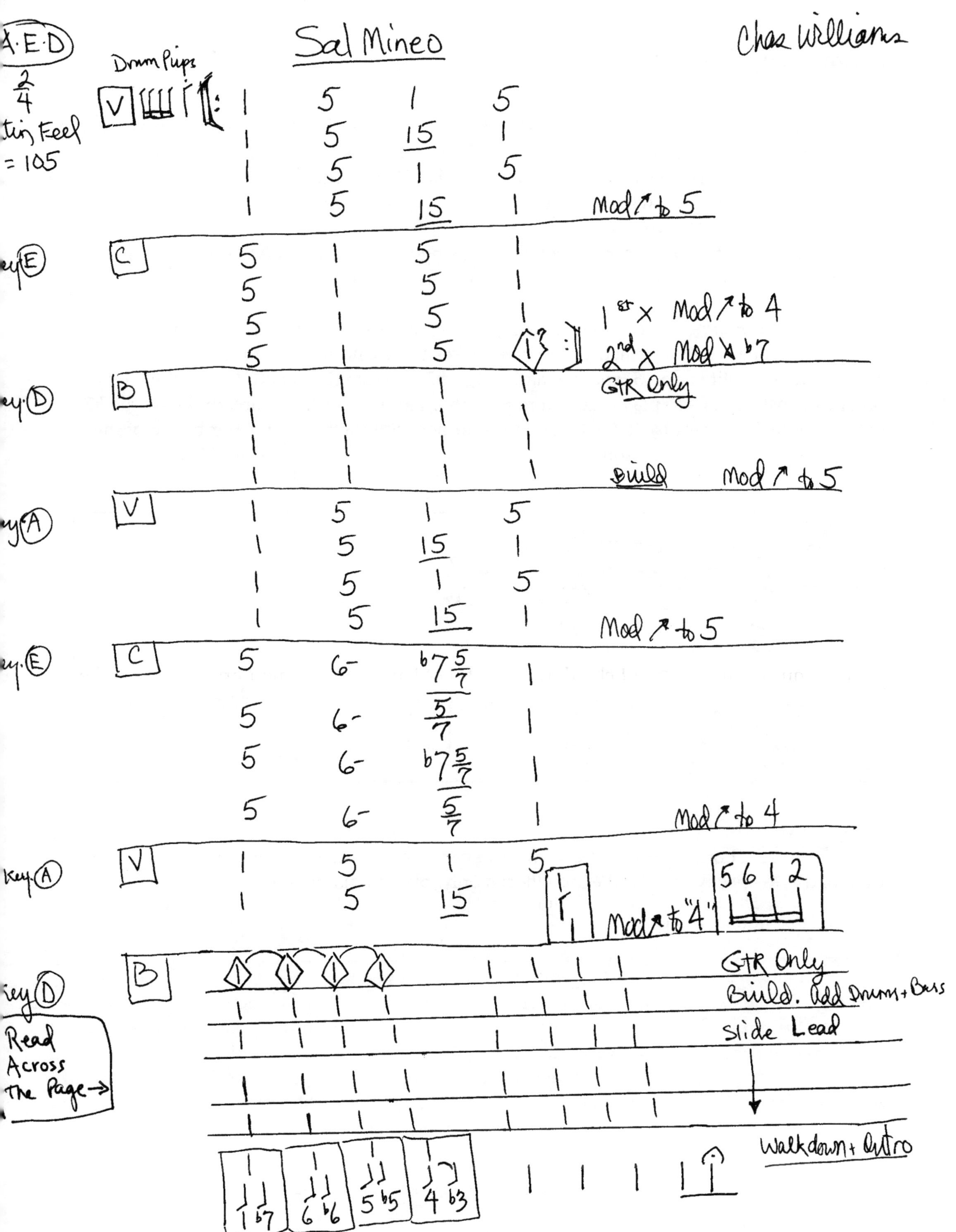
Sal Mineo
Chas Williams
A·E·D
Drum Pups
Mod ↗ to 5
1st X Mod ↗ to 4
2nd X Mod ↘ b7
GTR Only
Build
Mod ↗ to 5
Mod ↗ to 5
Mod ↗ to 4
Mod ↗ to "4"
GTR Only
Build. Add Drums + Bass
Slide Lead
Read Across The Page →
Walkdown + Outro

Sugar Notch

Sugar Notch is a fairly simple bluegrass tune with a swing feel. The chart is written in 2/4 and played with a 2/4 feel for the Verses. The back beats are on the "and" of beats 1 and 2 ; as you can hear on the snare. When we get to the Chorus, the 2/4 intensity breaks down to a mellower half time feel, with backbeats on beat 2 of each measure.

After the 1st Chorus repeat to the Verse using the 1st ending. After the 2nd Chorus, skip ending #1, play ending #2, and continue into the Bridge.

Look at *Figure 71* for a second. As you see, there are 3 bars of the **5** chord with diamonds, and all are tied together. The player strikes the **5** and holds it for all 3 bars, or 6 beats. Then there is a split bar of **5** and a small script ***b7***. I wrote the small ***b7*** for the bass and other low instruments to play a unison note without a full chord. We already know the ***b7*** gets a quarter note because it's in an evenly split bar with the **5** chord. After bar 16 of the Bridge comes the "Band Unison Lick", then on to the fiddle solo in the 3rd Verse.

Figure 71

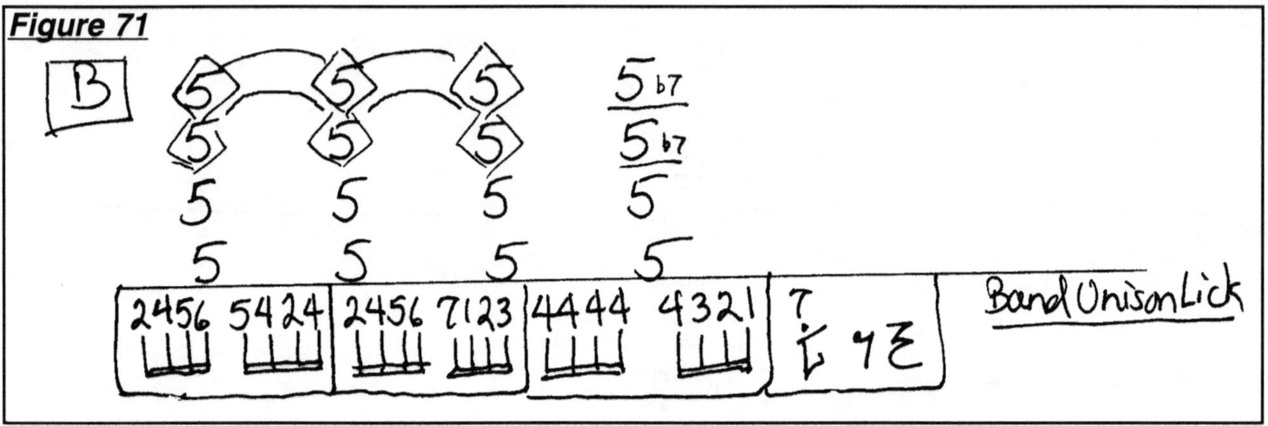

The 3rd Chorus really breaks down to everyone playing diamonds, so I wrote "1st X diamonds" to specify that for the 3rd Chorus only, players diamond each bar.

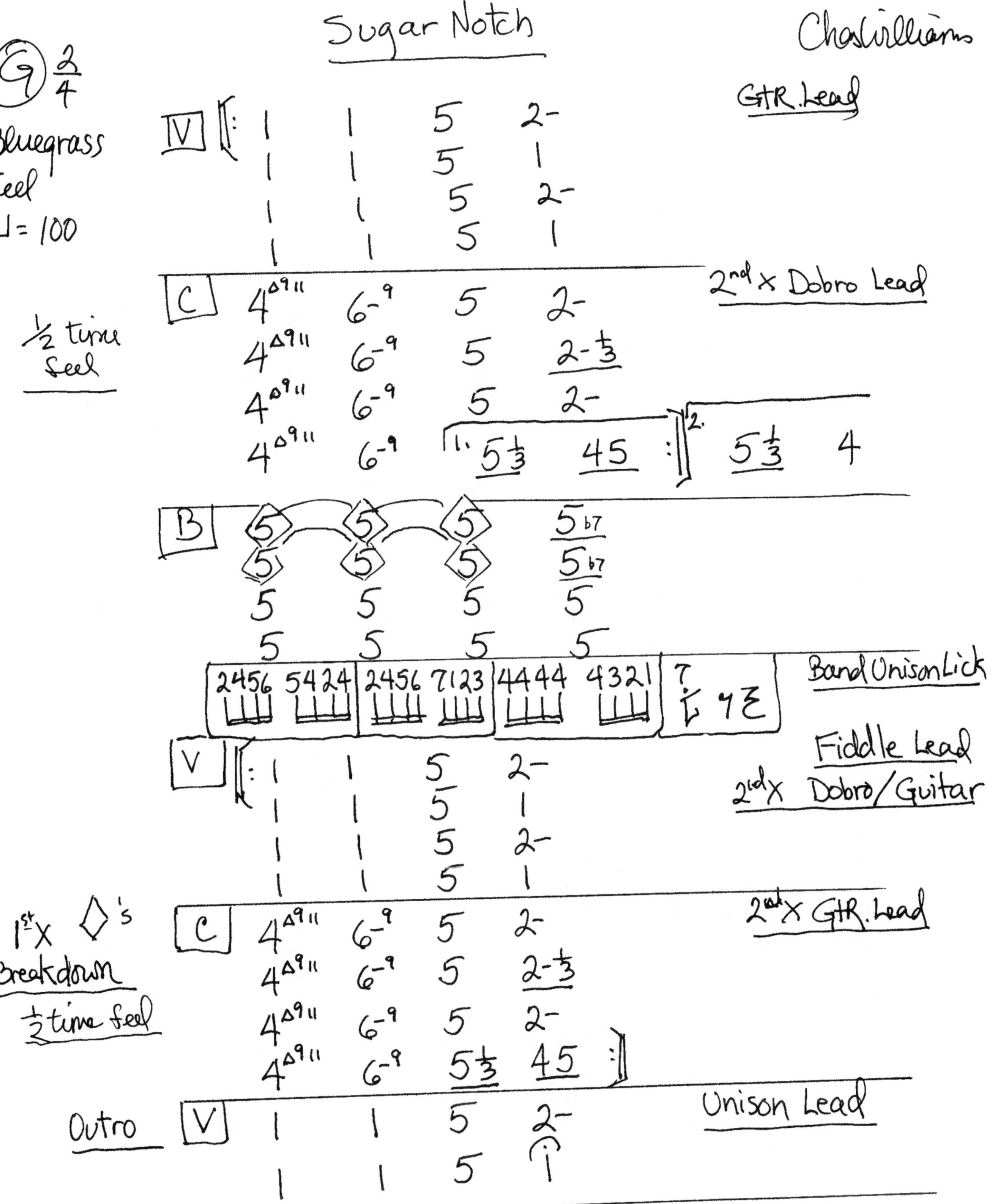
Sugar Notch
Chas Williams
G 2/4
Bluegrass Feel
♩= 100
GTR. Lead
IV
C
2nd X Dobro Lead
1/2 time feel
B
Band Unison Lick
2456 5424 2456 7123 4444 4321
V
Fiddle Lead
2nd X Dobro/Guitar
1st X ◊'s Breakdown
1/2 time feel
2nd X GTR. Lead
Outro
Unison Lead

Civil War

Ok, this one is kind of a long song. Because there are so many sections, instead of labelling Verses and Choruses, I'm calling them Sections A, B, C ... etc.

Civil War starts with 2 bars of marching snare drum. In the A section, like in the previous chart for Slide Guitar, uneven split bars have 2 hash marks over the chord that gets 2 beats. In 4/4 time, that leaves 2 beats to be distributed across the measure. Unless shown otherwise, the remaining 2 chords will each get 1 beat. Bar 8 of the A section is a 2/4 bar and bar 9 would be called, *"A Two seventh diamond, split One over Three, with three beats on the Two chord"*.

In the B section, there are simple eighth note pushes on the second half of bars 1, 3, 5 and 7. Bar 7 is a little more complex, however, so I wrote out the rhythmic figure. Bar 9 of this section has a 2 beat, **4** diamond, then a unison lick that helps us modulate up to the **6-** in the key of *F* for the C section.

The C section has definite action that I notated for the rhythm section. You don't have to notate every rhythmic figure, and I'm sure that upon hearing this song, players would probably make their own notations concerning this section. However, this is what it could look like if you did write it out.

At the end of the C section is a repeat sign, but no 1st and 2nd endings. So, you play everything within the repeats twice, then play the *"Six diamond split sharp four over sharp six diamond"*.

As you listen to the D section, notice how the guitar plays chord changes over a **6** in the bass. The bass player is pedalling the **6** and no one else is playing chord changes until the second guitarist joins in at the top of line 3. For line 4, the bass joins with the chord changes. Bar 17 of the D section is a pretty typical harmonization for a walk up to a **5** chord.

In the E section, things perk up quite a bit. First, we change time signature from 4/4 to Cut Time. So, a quarter note now equals 188 bpm. The bars will be going by quickly since we're counting each bar twice as fast. You can count this section in 2 with half notes at 94 bpm, but do you see how the *cut time* signature will be a little easier to read. Players will be reading quarter notes instead of sixteenth's. A quarter note push sign will be alot easier to feel than a sixteenth.

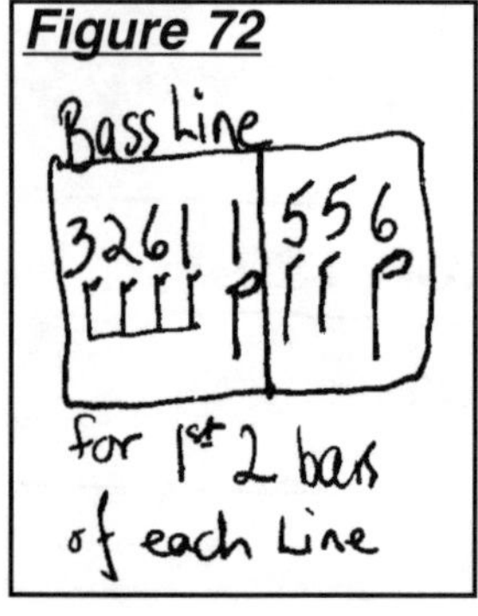

Figure 72 is a 2 bar phrase which I wrote out for the bass player to play on the 1st two bars of each line through section E.

Notice in the 2nd ending of the E section, a tied diamond of *"One over Four"*, then a 2 bar single note unison lick, still in cut time. After the unison lick, we change time signature back to the original 4/4 with the 8ths, ballad feel at 94 bpm in order to play the last A section.

Civil War p.2

The A, B and C sections on page 2 are identical to those at the beginning of the song. However, there are no repeats, but a modulation to a new section, F. Again, we change time signature; this time, we're playing in 2/4 with a Celtic fiddle tune feel. A quarter note still equals 94 bpm but there are only 2 of them per bar, so the bars will be going by twice as fast, just like they did in the E section. You would count, "One and two and,"at 94 bpm for one bar of 2/4. Notice how the band is pedalling on ***1*** through the Intro and 1st F section. No one plays chord changes until the walkdown at the last 2 bars of section F.

Finally, the band breaks down to guitar alone, then builds back up with repeats around sections F and G. The players vamp through these 2 sections until the fade.

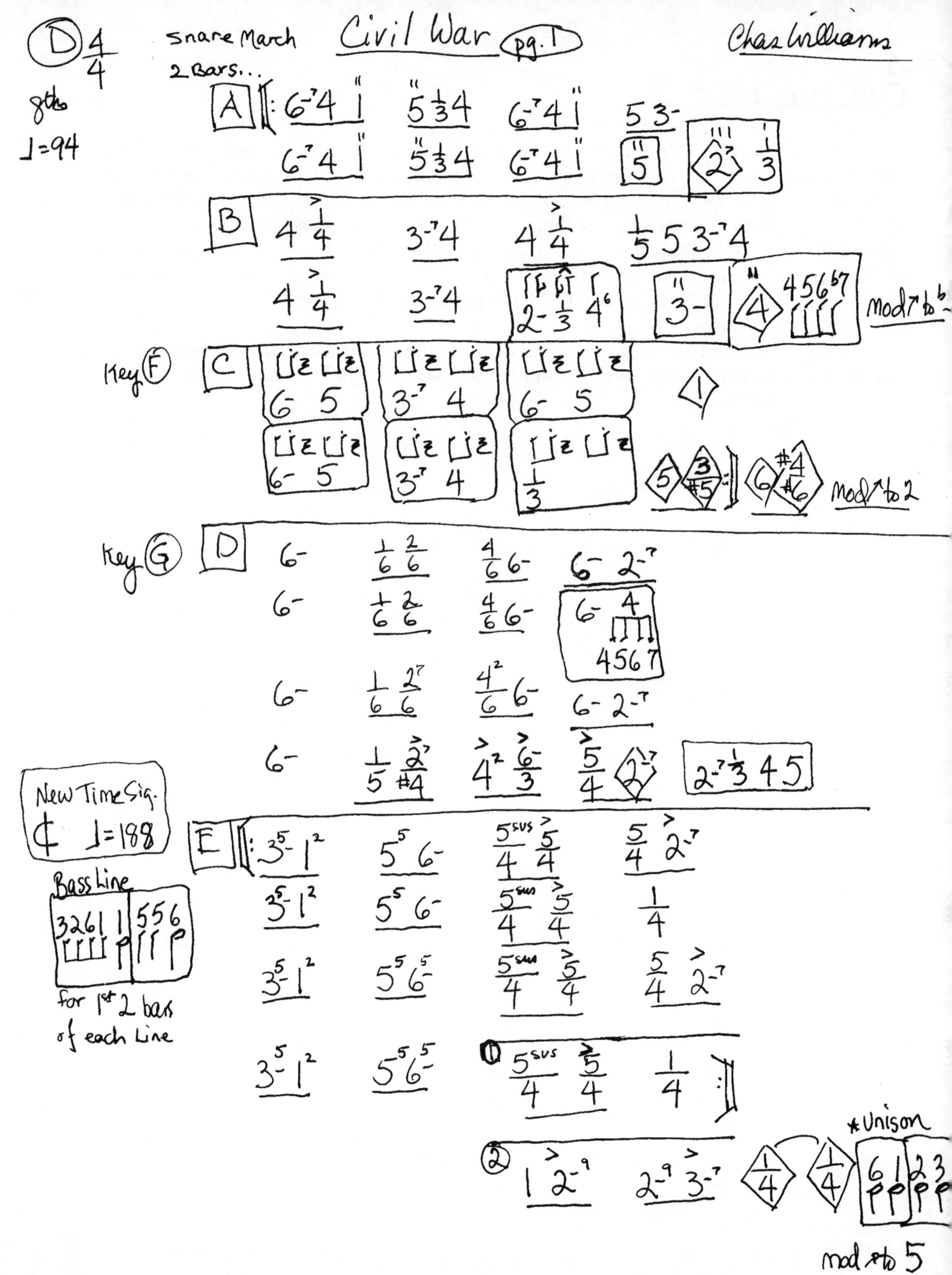
D 4/4
Snare March
Civil War pg. 1
Chas Williams
2 Bars...
8ths
♩=94
A
B
mod to b
Key F
C
mod to 2
Key G
D
New Time Sig.
¢ ♩=188
E
Bass Line
for 1st 2 bars of each Line
*Unison
mod to 5

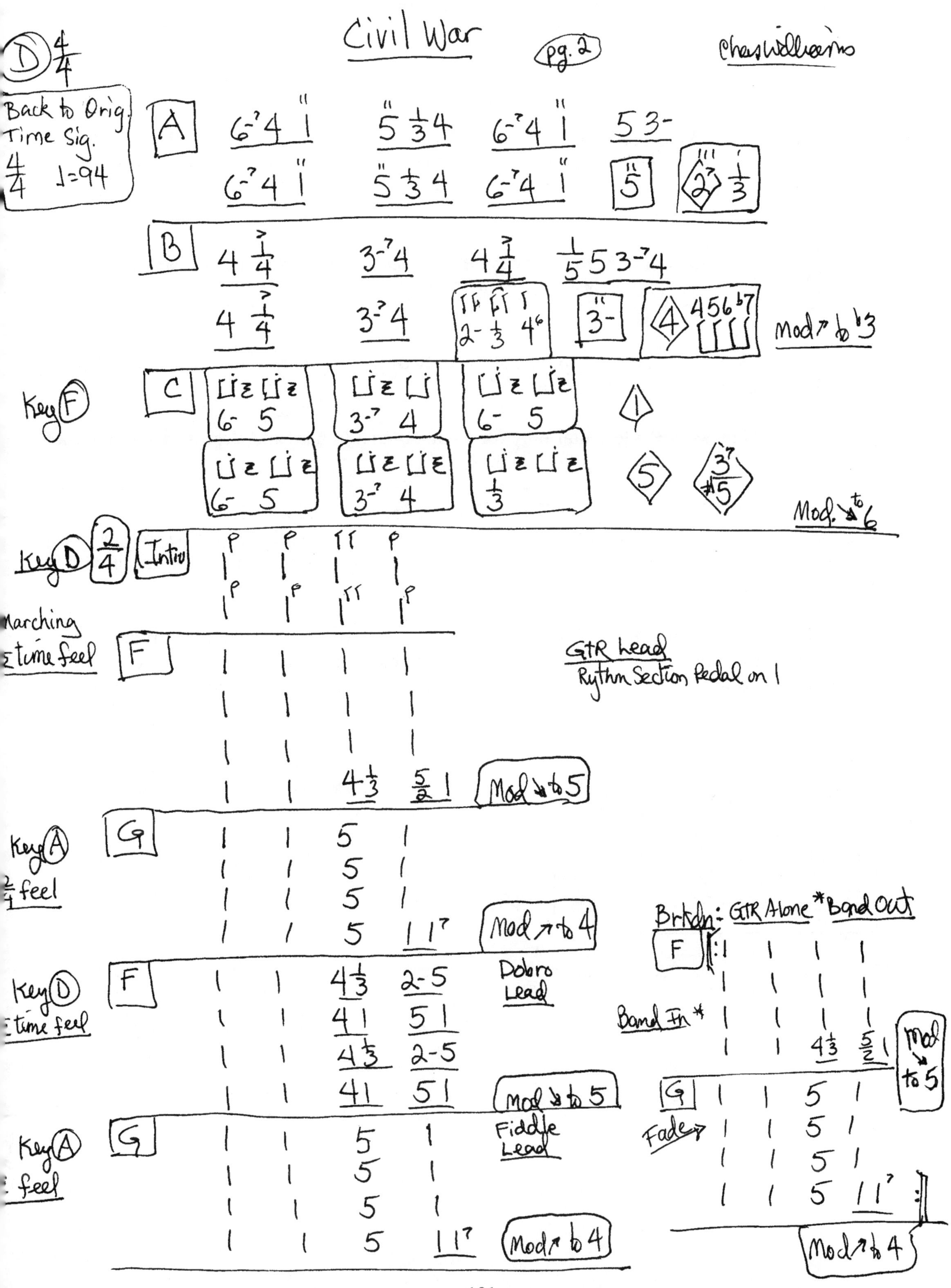
Civil War
pg. 2
Chas Williams
Back to Orig. Time Sig.
4/4 ♩=94
Mod to b3
Key F
Mod. to 6
Key D
Intro
Marching time feel
GTR Lead
Rythm Section Pedal on 1
Mod to 5
Key A
feel
Mod to 4
Brkdn: GTR Alone *Band Out
Dobro Lead
time feel
Band In*
Mod to 5
Fiddle Lead
Fade
Mod to 4

Gulf Coast

Gulf Coast is kind of a rock song with acoustic instruments. The guitar plays alone on the 1st Verse, then the band enters on the Chorus. The lead guitar is pushing a few beats, but this chart is primarily for the rhythm sections benefit. So I've marked pushes only where the band pushes together.

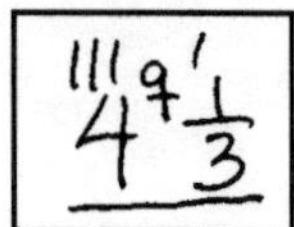

Also in the Chorus is my symbol for *add 9*. This bar would be called a ,*"Four add nine, split One over Three; with three beats on the Four."*

The 1st Verse and Chorus repeat, but the only difference in the 2 endings is that there is no rhythmic figure on the 2nd ending.

Verse 3 breaks down to guitar only for 4 bars, then add bass and drums on bar 5 of the section and the rest of the band enters at Chorus 3.

Notice that Chorus 3 only has 7 bars. The last bar of this Chorus is also the 1st bar of the 2nd Bridge. Since the *"Flat Six major nine, split flat seven; with pushes on both chords."* is the beginning of the musical phrase of the Bridge, I'm placing it with the Bridge instead of with the 3rd Chorus.

The band is soloing through the last Bridge and Outro. There is a rythmic figure on the last **4** chord (*Figure 73*), then a band unison lick which only lasts half a measure. I borrowed Lura Foster's double slanted line to show there was nothing to be played after the last note.

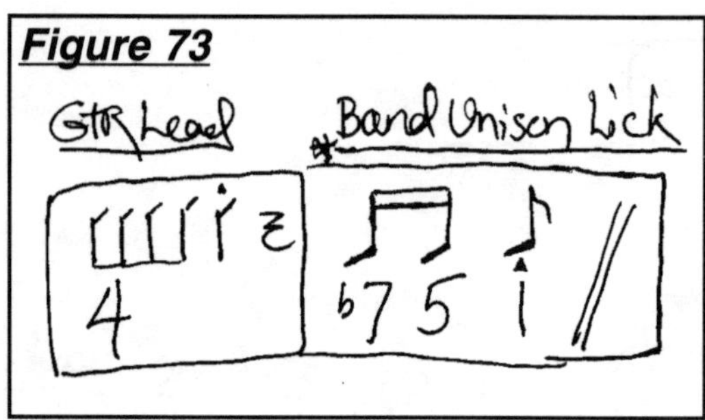

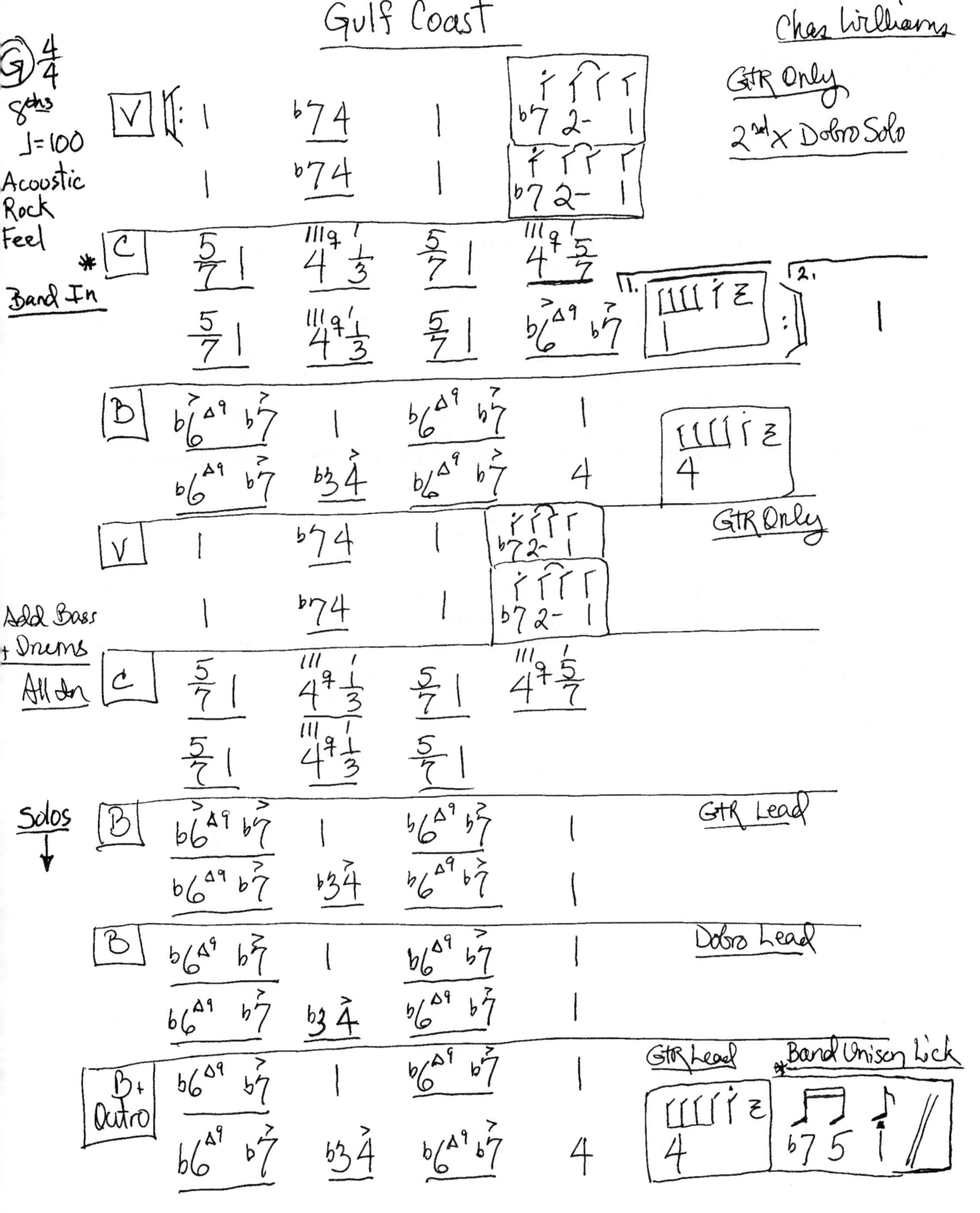
Gulf Coast
Chas Williams
G 4/4
8ths
♩=100
Acoustic Rock Feel
V
GTR Only
2nd x Dobro Solo
C
Band In
B
V
GTR Only
Add Bass + Drums
All In
C
Solos
B
GTR Lead
B
Dobro Lead
B + Outro
GTR Lead
Band Unison Lick

The Shuffle Board

I tried to write a simple song with only 3 chords, but it's way easier said than done. Well, this one has a simple 2 beat shuffle groove anyway. Again... modulating all over the place, so numbers are good; just so you know what key you're in.

The Shuffle Board chart is pretty staightforward until we get to the Chorus. After bar 6 of the Chorus, the song modulates down to the ***b7*** . The Chorus is in the key of E until the last 2 bars, which are in the key of D. Also, the following section is in the key of D. Modulating in the middle of a section like I did can look confusing. But if I stayed in E, the last 2 bars would have been : ***5 - b3 b7 4*** . Actually, these 2 bars are functioning in the key of D as: ***6 - 4 1 5*** . If a musician is having to figure out a harmony part or play fills, it would be easier to look at chords and analyse them diatonically. In other words, the phrase played over: ***6 - 4 1 5*** is from the D major scale. Otherwise, the same phrase over : ***5- b3 b7 4*** is a little more complicated to describe. If you play along with this chart, I think you'll come to the same conclusion.

Repeat the 1st Verse and Chorus, and the chart works it's way down to the 3rd Chorus with no new problems. Then look how we have 2 Choruses back to back. Well, I originally contradicted myself and wrote the last 2 bars of the 3rd Chorus as : ***5 - b3 b7 4*** . For one thing, we aren't going back to the key of D. The next Chorus stays in the key of E . So, I thought it would be too busy to have to modulate for 2 bars, then modulate back. Having said that, I guess, if you're reading this chart for the first time, the ***5 - b3 b7 4*** coming out of nowhere would throw anyone for a loop. By this time, we know what the musical figure is at the end of the Chorus, so every time you see that mod, you expect the figure to be the same as it has been the rest of the song. So, if we mod consistently each time, all the Choruses will look the same. The less a player has to think, the more he can concentrate on playing music.

The Shuffle Board

D 4/4
2 Beat Shuffle
♩=114

I 1/6 5

V ||: 1 6- 5 1 6- 5 4   2nd x Dobro Lead
1 6- 5 1 6- 5 4
3- 1 2/#4 5   2nd x Steel Lead
3- 1 2/#4 [5 6] Mod ↑ to "2"

(E) C 1 5 2-4 1 5 2-4   2nd x Dobro Lead
1 5 2-4 Mod ↓ to "b7" 6-4 1 5 :||

(D) B 4 b7⁹ 1 5 b7⁹ 1 6-5   GTR Lead
4 b7⁹ 1 5 b7⁹ 1 6- 5 5

V 1 6- 5 1 6- 5 4
1 6- 5 1 6- 5 4
3- 1 2/#4 5
3- 1 2/#4 [5 6] Mod ↑ to "2"

(E) C 1 5 2-4 1 5 2-4
1 5 2-4 Mod ↓ to "b7" 6-4 1 5 Mod ↑ to "2"

C 1 5 2-4 1 5 2-4
1 5 2-4 Mod ↓ to "b7" 6-4 1 5

(D) TAG 6-4 1 5 1
Rif

Northern Pike

Northern Pike is counted with 6 quarter notes per bar. The back beats fall on beat 4. Here is an example of a song with an obvious minor feel, written in it's relative major key. F is the relative major of D minor. The Verse could have been written in D minor, where the first 2 bars would be $1 -\ \ b7^{6}\ \ b6\ \ 5^{7}$. However, everytime we get to the Chorus, we'd have to modulate up to the relative major. For this reason, and the fact that *The Nashville Number System* is based on the major scale, most Nashville charts are written in a minor key's relative major.

The Intro is really not so much an Intro as it is 1 bar of pick up notes into the Verse, played in unison.

The 1st ending before the repeat sign is the same unison lick as played at the Intro. After the 2nd ending, we mod up to the ***4*** of the key of F for the Bridge. We're now in Bb. The 1st bar of the Bridge is a ***4 major 9*** or ***Eb major 9.***

After bar 7 of the Bridge, we mod down to the ***5*** of our Bridge key and play the Intro unison lick that takes us back to a Verse.

After Verse 3, there are 2 Choruses back to back, then we mod back up to the Bridge key of Bb.

Bridge 2 repeats 3X's as shown in Figure 74. The 1st 3 endings are all the same. Then, ending #4 is the same unison lick that has shown up so many times earlier in this song. A birdseye over the last chord, and the band holds it out until someone gives the cut off signal.

Figure 74

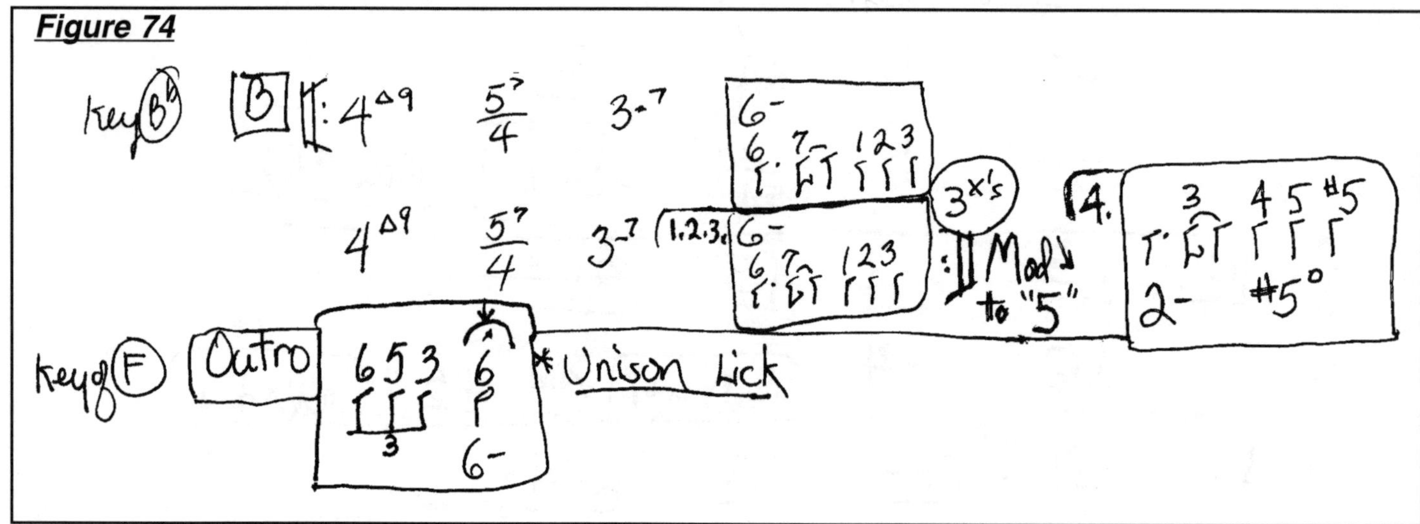

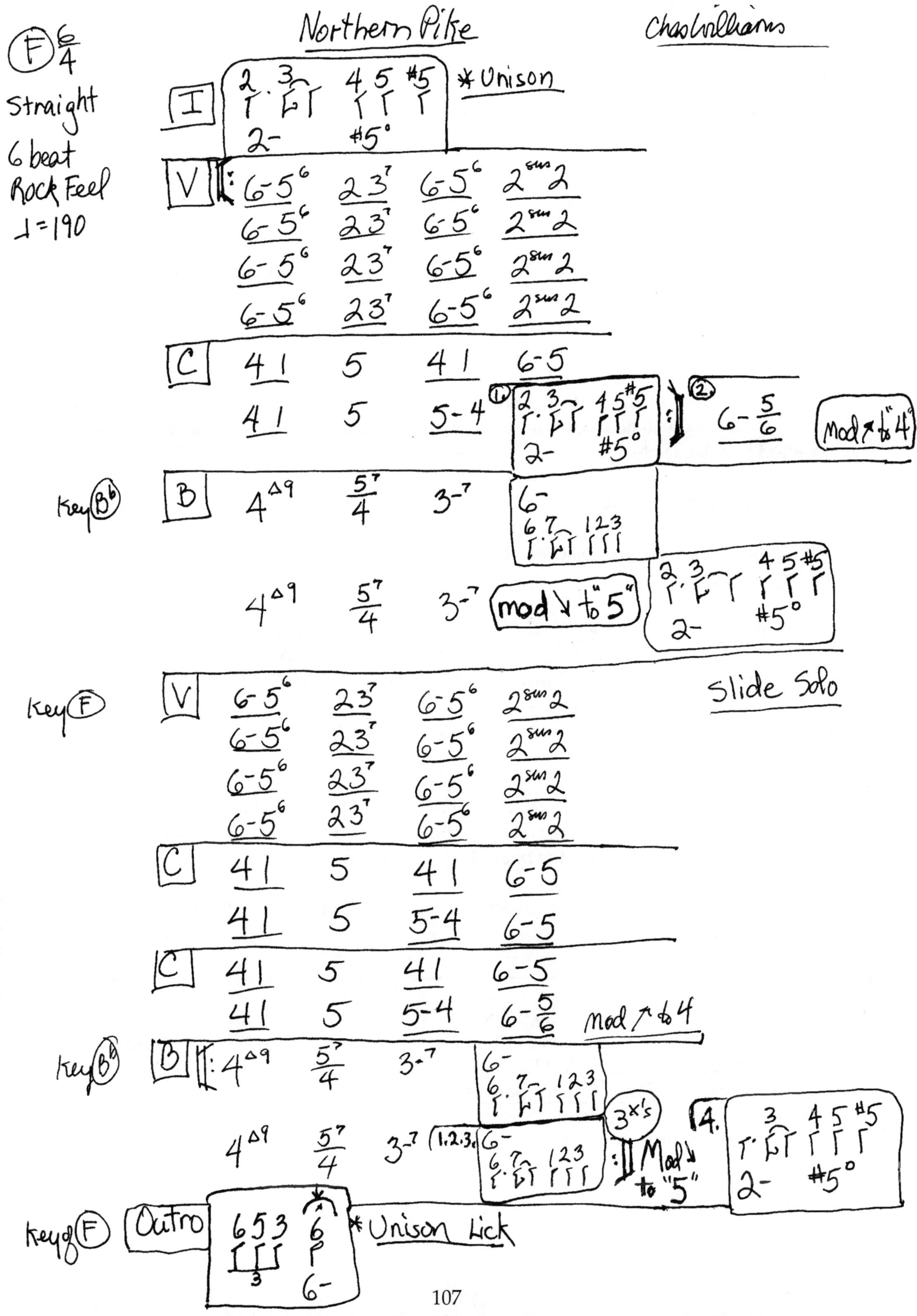

Northern Pike
Chas Williams
F 6/4
Straight 6 beat Rock Feel
♩=190
I
*Unison
V
C
mod ↗ to "4"
Key B♭
B
mod ↘ to "5"
Key F
Slide Solo
mod ↗ to 4
3x's
Mod ↘ to "5"
Key of F
Outro
*Unison Lick

Common Mistakes

The basics for good charts are: Key, Key Signature, Tempo, Feel, and Numbers in correct structure. If in doubt, stick to the basics.

The ***1*** chord is not necessarily the first chord of the song. Make sure you know what key you're in before you label the ***1*** chord.

Find out what your chords are. For example, $1^{maj\,7}$ is totally different from $\boldsymbol{1}^7$.

There is no such thing as a ♯***3*** or a ♯***7*** chord. Also, many people accidentally write a ***7*** when they mean a ♭***7***.

If you're a bass player, make sure to identify your chords. A "7" note to you could be a $\frac{5}{7}$ or $\frac{1}{7}$ chord, and the rest of the band will need to know. Also, be sure to identify major and minor even though it may not affect your bass note.

Complex arranging is not always best. For instance if there is a rhythm guitar lick that you do on the ***1*** chord, it may not be important that the whole band do the lick. Just write a ***1***, and show the guitar player the lick instead of writing complex notation that the rest of the band doesn't need to worry about.

The *D.S.* ***al*** ⊕ can be a time saver when writing a chart, but make sure you're not adding a degree of difficulty for those playing the chart. It's also difficult to read a chart with just one verse and chorus and a whole list of instructions for the structure of the song. Usually, it's just about as easy to write out the whole chart. That way, you can easily assign fills for different sections. Also, if a player gets lost for a second, he can quickly find his place at the top of the next section

Write your chart to emphasize phrasing. A line does not have to be 4 measures. An extra measure used for a breath at the end of a lyrical phrase should be written at the end of that line. Start the next line of the chart with the beginning of a new phrase.

Finally, the best way to avoid an incorrect chart is play it yourself before you give it to someone else to play.

Thanks:

Andy Most and all my friends who helped me with their musical knowledge.
Arnie Berle's Complete Handbook For Jazz Improvisation. Amsco Music Publishing Co.
A Modern Method For Guitar, Vol.I&II by William Leavitt. Berklee Press Publications.
Harrianne Condra at Sony/Tree for permission to use their songs.
Fishman Acoustic Amplification.
My wife Kathleen for putting up with me.

Additional Copies:

Check out the NNS Website: www.nashvillenumbersystem.com